Individual Values
and
Global Sharing

Individual Values
and
Global Sharing

Earl R. Brubaker

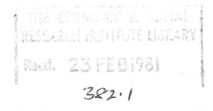

New York University Press · New York *and* London

Library of Congress Cataloging in Publication Data

Brubaker, Earl.
  Individual values and global sharing.

  Bibliography: p.
  Includes index.
  1. International agencies–Finance.
  2. International economic relations. I. Title.
  JX1995.B78   341.2   80-15874
  ISBN 0-8147-1031-X

Manufactured in the United States of America

Preface

International institutions for sharing global public programs normally are analyzed from a perspective entirely different from that adopted in this book. More than usual its purpose is to provoke thought and rational discussion rather than to pretend to definitive answers to admittedly especially intractable problems. Scholarly attention to many of the issues touched upon is in its infancy, so that the work is of necessity predominantly exploratory and tentative. Yet the problems it addresses are pressing, and current responses seem manifestly inadequate. The book is founded in the faith that scholarship and rational discourse can have a more prominent role in approaching more satisfactory solutions.

The author may be perceived as sympathetic to steps toward strengthening international organization, or even world governments and as insensitive to the dangers of a potentially oppressive global collectivism. But, in fact, the primary concern is for promoting meaningful individual participation to facilitate more rational decisions about globally collective purposes while avoiding impositions by the ultimate in remote, inaccessible (however well intentioned) centralized authority.

The intellectual debts incurred, simultaneously larger and more diverse than normal, will be evident throughout. Contributions from the modern theory of public choice and collective microeconomics, analyses of the nature and functions of international organizations, and the technical reports grappling with the latter's financial "crises" all contributed fundamentally to the present work.

The University of Wisconsin, its Department of Economics in particular, has provided a congenial, tolerant, and stimulating atmosphere for scholarly endeavor. W. Lee Hansen and John Culbertson read an early draft and provided valuable understanding and encouragement. An anonymous referee for New York University Press provided helpful comments both general and specific. Permission from the Peace Science Division of the World Friends Research Center and from the University of Wisconsin Press to incorporate material previously published in The *Journal of Peace Science* and *International Organization* is gratefully acknowledged.

Finally, this work has deep roots in schools, teachers, colleagues, friends, and family, tangled beyond human comprehension. It must be noted, nevertheless, that my wife, Svetlana Punkt Brubaker, listened to every word, more than once, with incredible patience and cheerful support.

Contents

Tables

CHAPTER I

Introduction

In the latter part of the twentieth century the emergence of worldwide economic interdependence has become ever more evident.[1] Undeniably complex, it takes a variety of forms. Most familiar is the mutual dependence created by sharing the gains from transnational specialization and exchange of privately owned goods. Substantial transnational exchanges create, in turn, an environment in which national economic policies and outcomes are inextricably intertwined. Given the great modern mobility of commodities, labor, real capital, and financial instruments, national monetary, fiscal, and regulatory policies, although ostensibly domestic, often have unintended influence, welcome or unwelcome, on attainment of targets elsewhere. A vast, perceptive, and highly useful set of studies on economic theory and policy facilitating rational choice of frameworks to cope with such forms of interdependence already exists.

Less prominent but also of potentially great significance is a rather different variety of worldwide economic interdependence, namely that created by sharing[2] globally benefits generated from certain programs and activities.[3] Many examples can be cited. For instance, casual impressions suggest a rather intense and widespread desire on the part of individual human beings for law, order, and justice in the international community as well as in their more immediate surroundings. A common desire for control of international terrorism and crime constitutes a bond

1

among the overwhelming majority of mankind. War is feared even by those not directly involved because of the danger of subsequent entanglement and because of potential spread of lethal or other noxious materials to nonparticipants. Humanitarian impulses also constitute a motive for support of multilateral efforts to ameliorate and control intergovernmental conflicts. The potential benefit of international programs for controlling political and governmentally inspired violence generally seem to be very widely accepted.

Transfers of income to alleviate the calamity of starvation, or indeed of less pressing poverty and deprivation in the world community, tend to benefit persons of goodwill everywhere. Joint projects for protection from physical spillover effects like those associated with test explosions of fissionable materials, dumping of industrial wastes, accumulations of pesticides, herbicides, and so on, or those associated with ruinous rivalry in the exploitation of common property resources may be cited. Production and distribution of basic knowledge produce benefits ever more rapidly transformed into a common asset held simultaneously by a large part of all mankind.[4]

Further strengthening of transnational interdependencies seems inevitable. Interactions and interconnections, barring major unanticipated departures from recent trends, will multiply (Katzenstein). Areas of common interest will expand. Ties will become firmer with the further progress of transportation, communications, and economic development generally. Equally inevitable are innovation and adaptation of decision-making mechanisms where interdependencies are manifest. The calls for a "new international economic order" heard so persistently since the mid-1970s seem at least partly due to growing realization of the need to adapt international arrangements in accord with the emerging technological and economic realities.

The fundamental objective of this book is to analyze global sharing.[5] Special attention will be paid to interrelationships between relevant concepts of efficiency and equity, mechanisms intended to promote their attainment, and the implications of individual values and behavior for determining actual results. To attain these general objectives, a whole series of more specific issues must, of course, be addressed.

For example, is global sharing a purely political problem, as most previous scholarly work maintains, or does it have significant dimensions amenable to meaningful economic analysis? Great appreciation for fundamental insights provided by received doctrine clearly need not preclude approach from a rather different methodological perspective. Thus, the present work is inspired largely by the presumption that modern economic theory[6] has much to contribute to understanding the problems and possibilities of sharing, including that of ultimate scope. Normative economic models stating conditions for optimal allocation to public programs generally can be applied to international public goods. Such models demonstrate the importance of taking strict account of individual values to define the optimum. Current doctrine also emphasizes, however, that optimality conditions tell nothing about the methods likely to be most effective in obtaining requisite revenues. In fact, it calls attention to lack of personal material incentives to reveal demands with the resulting danger of free-riding and grossly suboptimal revenues. These general propositions seem quite consistent with perceived difficulties in obtaining "adequate" revenues for international programs.

On the other hand, progress in the general theory of demand for public programs has increased significantly its applicability to problems associated with obtaining revenue for the transnational variety.[7] In particular, orthodox analysis had been limited by strict adherence to the proposition that assessments backed by the coercive police power of the state, the traditional means for raising revenues to expend on collective items, are both possible and appropriate. While the relevance of this proposition to goods collective only at lower levels of jurisdiction may be challenged, its usefulness is particularly suspect where the ultimate in centralization is concerned. Possibilities for financing worldwide public consumption on a voluntary basis have increased with rising knowledge of the circumstances under which individuals may be willing to express latent demands. Whereas a few years ago there was a nearly universal consensus that voluntary collective action would be ineffective, recent studies provide much greater grounds for optimism regarding ability to contrive terms leading to expression of substantial demand for pure public goods by individuals in a large group.

Finally, traditional microtheoretic analysis calls attention to the potential prohibitive transactions cost where a large number of persons must, in effect, reach agreement on the appropriate extent of a public program. Statement of this problem has inspired analysis of intermediaries' ability to facilitate relevant negotiations and contracts. Clearly, the collection and collation of data relevant to sharing globally public programs will be a formidable task. A vital component of any mechanism for promoting such programs will be a legitimized global collective-good intermediary (GCGI) possessing channels of communication with an overwhelming majority of potential individual beneficiaries.

Another crucial question for any analysis of universally collective goods is whether in fact demands for them exist in any significant amount. In the current state of relevant theory and practice, it would be presumptuous, if not foolhardy, to claim that we can estimate with any great accuracy and confidence the extent of such demands. But given their potentially worldwide scope, and consequently potentially quite substantial magnitude, an examination of currently available evidence providing even elemental indications promises an important contribution to understanding these vital phenomenona.

One prominent indication is the frequent reference to "needs" for international public progams. Since 1945, responding to expressions of such need, over fifty nations have participated in a variety of peacekeeping operations undertaken by the United Nations in such disparate parts of the world as Greece, Palestine, Indonesia, Kashmir, Egypt, Lebanon, the Congo, West Irian, Yemen, Cyprus, India and Pakistan, and the Suez Canal zone. On a number of other occasions, the potential benefit from international peacekeeping, in Cambodia, Vietnam, and Zimbabwe, to cite a few outstanding examples, was widely articulated, even if unrealized. Perceived needs for multinational joint efforts for alleviating the most distressing poverty were reflected directly in the UN General Assembly's establishment of the Expanded Programme of Technical Assistance in 1949, the United Nations Special Fund in 1958, and the United Nations Development Programme in 1966. In the mid-1970s the General Assembly's resolutions, entitled "Declaration on the Establishment of a New International Economic Order," the "Charter of Economic Rights and Duties of States," and "Development and International Economic Cooperation" constituted more urgent expressions of the need for international income transfers in one form or another. Still another set of needs, worldwide in scope, is reflected in the relatively recently established UN Environment Programme. As Elmandjra states, "The protection of the national natural and physical environment is no longer entirely subject to national control measures. It now requires internationally coordinated programs as well as sets of international norms and policies" (p. 313). Steinberg, Yager and Brannon likewise argue that such needs are great and growing (p. 15).

Expressions of perceived needs in the forms described above are, of course, only loosely indicative of the possibility that substantial demands exist or may arise in the near future. But even now the case for their existence, based as it is on fragmentary evidence and precursory analysis, seems sufficiently promising to warrant devoting considerably greater effort to more precise and reliable measures.

Undoubtedly still another issue essential to analysis of global sharing must be the relations among alternative institutions, mechanisms, policies, and procedures, and the degree of individual demand disclosures. Certainly a decisive role for institutions cannot be ruled out. For instance, relatively meager funds channeled through the United Nations for peacekeeping very well may reflect the organization's *ban* on personal contributions rather than human predilections for free-riding. This ban on international organization programs for orderly pursuit of justice (IOPOPJ) [8] appears bizarre form the perspective of modern microeconomics, since *overcoming* obstacles to accurate revelations of demand, not *creating* them, has been its primary concern. But, of course, the ban on personal contributions for peacemaking is only an extreme example. A large variety of institutions and policies to arrange for global sharing has been employed or proposed. A systematic evaluation of their potential for facilitating efficient and equitable results surely can contribute to understanding this vital subject.

The scope of the present work is limited in at least two ways. First, no detailed plan to raise large amounts of revenue is proposed. As Bruce K. Maclaury pointed out in his foreword to Steinberg et al.; *New Means of Financing International Needs,* such a plan undoubtedly would be premature. But on the other hand, studies to stimulate "concerned people in all parts of the world [to] think . . . about the steps that may have to be taken if growing international financial needs are to be met," may be due, if not overdue. Second, the general analytical approach is applied to only one kind of collective good, international security programs. Although the principles of public microeconomics promise eventually to contribute much to rational discussion of other collective goods as well, much work remains to be done. Undoubtedly the various globally public projects will be characterized by their own peculiar problems and considerations, which may call for qualifications to the general conclusions. A comprehensive analysis simply has not been feasible to date. [9] The current work is offered, therefore, as another step toward a more nearly definitive analysis.

In brief, the argument of the book is structured as follows. The cases for existence of an economic dimension to the "political" problem of global sharing and the relevance of the individualist postulate are presented in Chapter II. The basic collective microeconomic theoretical framework is elaborated in Chapter III. That framework provides the concepts and principles for analyzing: (1) traditional approaches to international cost sharing (Chapter IV); (2) experience of the United Nations (Chapter V); and (3) the experience of its specialized agencies and of international nongovernmental organizations (Chapter VI). Evidence relevant to judging how large demand for international peacekeeping might be is assembled and interpreted in Chapter VII. Previous proposals for reform are reviewed and evaluated in Chapter VIII with special attention to the pros and cons of voluntary, individual contributions. Finally, a reform inspired by a microeconomic, public choice perspective is presented in Chapter IX.

NOTES

1. For a very useful selected bibliography, see *International Organization* (Winter 1975), and for data on recent trends see Katzenstein.

2. In a less tangible yet very real way, the existence of an unrealized opportunity for sharing also constitutes a source of interdependence.

3. Prominent examples of relevant work include: Dosser (Kyklos) and *(Rev. Econ. and Stat.);* Dosser and Peacock; Herber; Kravis and Davenport; Musgrave and Musgrave; Olson and Zeckhauser; Padelford (10-15-62) and (10-26-62); Pincus; Price; Rosenstein-Rodan; Russett and Sullivan; Schelling; Steinberg, Yager, and Brannon; Stoessinger et al; and Taubenfeld and Taubenfeld.

4. Creation of basic knowledge involves still another more widely heralded aspect of interdependence. Increasing ease of communication and transportation has facilitated growth of transnational interactions promoting further progress of knowledge. Artists, scientists, scholars, and businessmen with common interests but different nationalities and native languages communicate more profusely and perhaps more effectively than ever before. The scope for mutually beneficial transnational exchange of concepts, interpretations, and opinions has expanded enormously.

The advance of basic knowledge also depends vitally, although indirectly, on the state of intergovernmental relations and on the national security programs adopted in consequence. Their impact on the physical sciences has been lamented on the one hand but lauded on the other. One might speculate that the impact on the humanities and social studies is more clear-cut. Knowledge of history and knowledge about the character and effects of political, economic, and social stystems has been severely retarded by anxieties of national leaders regarding their legitimacy or perhaps their place in history, and national security has been cited repeatly as justification for prolonged denial of free access to archives. In many cases individuals acting in the name of the state destroy evidence or prevent its creation in the first place.

5. Voluntary transnational associations of special-interest groups that can easily exlude nonmembers from the benefits created by the association, although also of considerable interest, are only on the fringe of the focus of the present inquiry.

6. A clearly nonexhaustive list of noteworthy recent contributions to the literature in English would include: Baumol; Buchanan; Margolis and Guitton; Musgrave (1959) and (1971); Musgrave and Peacock (1967); Olson; and Samuelson (1954) and (1955).

7. See, for examples and further citations to the literature, Bohm (1971) and (1972); Brubaker (1975a) and (1975b); Douty; Dreze and de la Vallee Poussin; Groves and Ledyard; and Mueller.

8. As roughly synonymous to IOPOPJ we might refer to international organizational programs for international order, security, peacekeeping and peacemaking; or for amelioration and control of conflict. Some scholars may find useful a distinction among these concepts. For present purposes it will not be necessary.

9. Employing a rather different analytical framework, Steinberg, Yager, and Brannon, for example, studied financing of international needs with special reference to environmental protection. Pincus focused on economic aid.

CHAPTER II

Is Global Sharing a Purely Political Problem?

Many of the most prominent historical experiences with global sharing have been arranged through the United Nations organization. Its problems with financing certain programs consequently might be viewed as indicative of general difficulties associated with sharing globally. But most authorities on financing the United Nations, like some early writers on *national* public finance, emphasized that its financial problem is not financial (or economic) at all but political, and much can be said for this point of view. Its case has been presented very effectively, and in the process many precious perceptions have been provided. There are, however, some extremely troublesome aspects to the analysis, and significant additional insights and some important new conclusions might be gained by approaching the matter from a rather different angle.

A. The Political-Economic Connection

In particular because of the integral relations between many political and economic phenomena, and because financing almost inevitably will at least touch upon some economic issues, an economic analysis may be very useful. Humans often pursue their ends by political *and* economic means. The intimate connection is readily apparent in the high evaluation of financial support by political protagonists, in the variety of eco-

8

nomic means for expressing "political" preferences, in the relationship between personal economic status and political outlook, and in the heavy economic policy content of many "political" programs.

The assertion that politicians often value financial support more highly than mere yeas or nays seems scarcely likely to provoke much controversy. Expressions of "political" will can take many forms beyond simply casting a ballot, campaigning, cajoling, bargaining, compromising, and so on. Perhaps just as important are donations of costly resources in support of candidates or issues. Furthermore, posting signs, writing or giving speeches, providing transportation for voters, delivering handbills, placing phone calls, and other such contributions in kind constitute economic affirmations of "political will" no less than financial contributions. Thus, assertions of political will can be accomplished not merely through voting or vocal support but also through making known intensities of preferences by forgoing other goods and services either directly in kind or indirectly through surrender of financial instruments. In other words, expressions of political preferences may be regarded as goods that compete with all others for an individual human being's scarce resources.

Personal political preferences often seem to be intimately related to economic status, and they often seem to derive ultimately from concerns about the character and level of governmental programs from which consumer benefits may be obtained and/or taxpayer costs may be incurred. Even where political preference is declared for a candidate or for the general rules of the game, the ultimate objective often, though of course not always, and perhaps subconsciously, is the individual's economic welfare. Political problems frequently involve economic motives and uses of scarce resources, either directly in the creation of public services, or indirectly through choices affected by policymakers or by the rules of the game. Political problems very often have significant economic dimensions, and an economic approach to their analysis may contribute significantly to rational responses. Extending this general line of reasoning to the financial problems of international organizations, we might be led to suspect that they, too, may have important economic as well as political dimensions.

It can scarcely be overemphasized that all of the above does not imply that the traditional, political view of financing international organizations must or should be scrapped. It means rather that international organizations can and do arrange for programs that create benefits for, and impose costs on, individuals. And it means that political and economic channels for expressing individual desires about the character and extent of international organizations' programs can and do coexist. Denial of one channel for input into the process of aggregating preferences may seriously reduce its overall effectiveness. It means that contemporary economic theory may have some useful contributions to make to decisions about the optimal (or appropriate) allocation of resources to international organizations. Specifically international organizations may contribute to efficient allocation of resources by facilitating creation of goods collective beyond the national, and perhaps at the global, level.

In sum, we shall argue that financing of programs creating benefits worldwide has an important economic dimension and that developments in the economic theory of public choice promise to add significantly to understanding and to effective practical arrangements for providing more nearly optimal revenues that international organizations need for their programs. This economic viewpoint will lead to some novel conclusions about the nature, significance, and appropriateness of alternative mechanisms for obtaining UN revenues.

B. Insights from the Political Approach

Before setting out on an exploration of the nature and implications of an economic approach, let us first review the essentials of the currently prevailing doctrine and the insights it has provided.[1] The proposition that the UN financial problem is in fact political stems in large part from the assumption that the United Nations is an institution of, by, and for its member states. It follows in turn that the answers to certain essential questions about the organization must be answered by national policymakers, that is, by the subset of individuals who occupy positions of authority at or close to the peak of the pyramid of national governmental apparatuses. What is the appropriate role for the United Nations? How should the cost of its operations be distributed among the membership? These are questions that are political in nature, to be decided by give-and-take, voting, bargaining, and compromise of relevant politicians.

Some of the major elements of this position are especially interesting and deserving of closer examination. In this view, the limited activities and financial straits of the United Nations merely have reflected the realities of the situation, namely, the low priority accorded to its operations by the relevant decision makers. The problem is not at all the lack of financial wherewithal but the lack of will to commit it to expansion of UN programs. The limited activities of general international agencies reflect a revelation of missing enthusiasm on the part of their membership. Financial support more accurately than mere words indicates policymakers' feeble commitment to the extension of activities for an international organization.

The appropriate role for the United Nations will be complex, and its path of development determined in incremental stages. Nevertheless, some boundaries may aid in steering along an optimal path. On one side, the organization's activities may be constrained to the minimum defined by the acquiescence of each and every member state. On the other, they may be extended so far as to generate outright opposition of certain national governments. Such opposition may entail negative consequences for the United Nations as well as for the direct relations among states potentially parties to conflict. Under these circumstances it is only prudent to stay very close to the unanimity boundary in the short term while planning and attempting to move that boundary outward to obtain unanimous consent for more ambitious activities in the longer term. It is recognized, moreover, that the boundaries may often be difficult to discern and that they may be exceedingly flexible. Thus, the risks of provoking opposition and dysfunctional conflict by crashing into such boundaries must be traded off against the risk of inadequate adoption of potentially beneficial programs because of excessive timidity.

Not only the appropriate programs and their levels but also the associated cost-sharing arrangements must be decided somehow. Conflicts over cost sharing may be avoided under some circumstances by relying on voluntary contributions. Conversely, controversy may be expected when attempts are made to assess members for support of programs independently of their own evaluation of the benefits. Thus, even if member states agree on services to be provided by the international organization, they may come into conflict over apportionment of costs. More specifically, they may differ over criteria for apportionment as well as over mechanisms for determining assessments. Ability to pay, universal participation, major power responsibility, guilty-party responsibility, and distribution of benefit are some of the criteria that have been advocated, and they provide ample scope for controversy in and of themselves. It has been asserted that the "most acceptable principle of cost-distribution for members of international organizations is that embodied in the scheme of voluntary contributions: that is, financial support should be correlated with political support; a state should give financial backing to an international activity only if and to the extent that it regards that activity as compatible with and conducive to the interests and purposes expressed in its national policy" (Stoessinger et al., p. 21). Sanctions that might be contemplated for use against a recalcitrant member state appear hardly promising. Most member states, unlike individual taxpayers, need not submit to the compulsion designed to induce their financial support for activities in which they perceive no good and perhaps some bad.

The issue of financing is intimately related to the question of control, or the locus of decision making, with regard to an organization's activities. No matter what the formal voting rules, withholding financial support can effectively curtail programs on the one hand. On the other, the role of contributor confers a correspondingly prominent role in their direction.

The political conception of the United Nations financing problem can serve as a foundation for predicting some consequences of a "financially independent" [2] organization. If in fact such independence were achieved, it might be expected to reduce controversy over the role of the UN executive. There would be fewer delays and less haggling over "fair shares." "States" perceiving essentially no benefit from a given activity would not be inclined to oppose it in order to avoid an assessment for a contribution to what they consider a worthless program. [3]

Although controversy may be reduced, it would not be eliminated through fiscal independence, and national governments opposed to specific programs could be expected to search for substitutes for the tactic of financial nonsupport. Given fiscal independence, the mechanism for initiating programs would become of greater significance and therefore a bone of contention.

Analysts inclined to favor fiscal independence for the United Nations argue that the organization would be better able to provide for collective needs on the international plane. It could move quickly to prevent escalation of international disputes to levels at which the risk of extremely irrational decisions became great, and it could mount more effective programs in support of economic development and elimination of human deprivation.

Others caution that financial independence might promote studied neglect on the part of national governments where international controversies were concerned. The United Nations might be relegated to engaging in programs inspiring relatively little conflict, but because of financial autonomy it would suffer reduced eminence as a tool of nations in their interactions with one another. They claim that "the dependence of the United Nations on the financial support of states may be essential to its being taken seriously by states; this dependence may weaken its executive effectiveness, but enhance its political meaningfulness" (Stoessinger et al., p. 33).

In sum, the political conception of the United Nations financial problem stresses that the UN is an intergovernmental organization and that its evolution must be ultimately decided by the appropriate authorities from the member nations. The financial difficulties of the UN are a consequence of attempting programs despite the opposition of a major member. In general, when an international organizational program arouses such opposition two clear-cut options emerge. The UN may yield to what is in effect a veto, or it may carry on undeterred. Compromise through modification of the activity is of course also possible. Especially in the longer-term, efforts to expand the space of minimal consensus for United Nations operations may prove worthwhile. In other words, "the constructive political approach is to explore and exploit the possibilities of convincing the dissident power that its own best interest requires an effectively operational United Nations and that the Organization can be relied on to render impartial service" (Stoessinger et al., p. 34). Such expansion of consensus cannot be expected to emerge abruptly. The range of activities tolerated, valued, or supported by the several member states may be extended gradually. Toward this intermediate goal, a constant testing and probing, "an expanding of the limits of political consensus might best reflect a policy of realism and vision" (Stoessinger et al., p. 34).

C. An Economic Approach

How can an economic approach contribute to understanding the fundamental issues of the "appropriate role" for the United Nations and of how the costs of its programs might be shared? This approach substitutes an alternative axiom for the assumption that the United Nations is an organization of, by, and for member states; namely, it emphasizes that the organization was created for the benefit of individual human beings and is operated and supported by individual human beings who ultimately share the benefits and the costs of the organization's programs. Activities arranged by the UN create benefits for individuals that can in some degree substitute for those that might be created through alternative potential uses of resources. The appropriate role for the United Nations can be described, therefore, in terms of an optimal level of activities reflecting a balance between the benefits as perceived by individuals and costs measured by alternative goods that need to be forgone.

1. INDIVIDUALIST POSTULATE

The viewpoint that we have just examined in outline reflects acceptance of the "individualist postulate," an axiom so basic for any collective choice that a more extended treatment of its meaning and its implications for choice in the international community is necessary here.[4]

Two basically differing points of departure for a theory of choice for collective goods have been identified, and they contribute much to understanding differences in the political and economic approaches to an appropriate role for international organizations. Specifically, a decision needs to be made at the outset regarding the role of the individual. The first approach takes the individual human being and his preferences as the elemental building blocks. Collective choices must be made with reference to such individual preferences. Collective goods as well as private create benefits only inasmuch as they satisfy the needs of some set of human beings, and efficient allocation of resources and distribution of output can be accomplished only by reference to such needs. The individualist postulate precludes neither some delegation of authority nor a degree of altruism. The essential requirement is that individual preferences, their idiosyncrasies, and their intensities be the ultimate inputs into the collective choice. Under this purely individualistic conception, it is true, some mechanism, set of rules, or procedure must be adopted that permits aggregation of individual preferences or, in other words, transformation of individual desires into collective support of a program. In this view, community representatives, international or national, constitute, in essence, collective-good intermediaries who aggregate the individual evaluations according to previously specified rules.[5]

There is no claim that even in theory all problems relevant to implementing the individualistic approach have been resolved. Any collective choice must reflect somehow the net result of a large number of individual preferences pulling and pushing with varying intensity in disparate directions, and the net result may depend in large part upon the institutions and mechanisms employed.

This approach emphasizes, then, that individuals make decisions and that therefore the actions of groups, whether they are local communities, states, provinces, nations, or an international organization, can be understood best by focusing on the preferences, incentives, and actions of individuals. An organization may be formed to promote a common objective, but group actions reflect the decisions of individual members. Individuals forgo other goods to secure the benefits provided by collective goods, and individuals therefore expect to contribute to judgments about the benefits provided by collective goods relative to opportunity costs.

2. ORGANIC CONCEPTION OF STATE

The second approach dispenses with the individual building blocks and proceeds directly to consider "social needs" as determined by an elite that "knows best" and can therefore make important allocation and distributional choices for the entire society. In other words, the primacy of individual preferences may be rejected for an organic conception of the state that postulates the discovery of an abstract general will that is not a function of the process through which collective choices are made. An elite subset of individuals discerns the path generating the greatest net benefit and is therefore entrusted to make choices for the community with limited obligation to consult individual opinions.

The mode of emergence of the elite clearly is a crucial issue. So are the issues of the criteria and methods by which the elite arrives at its decisions. Thorough, systematic considerations of the relative merits of these two approaches is well beyond the scope of the current analysis, but explicit recognition of the existence of such fundamentally different axioms may add significantly to clarity in the discussion of issues focused upon in this work.

Analysts of UN financing usually have not made an explicit choice, and a clear ambivalence is prominent in their work. Inclinations toward the individualist postulate do appear in the rejection of an organic conception of the United Nations. They see the organization as an agency of, by, and for the member states, owned and operated, so to speak, by them. The UN has no higher interest. Its outlook is compounded from preferences of individual states.

But here the application of the individualist conception ends abruptly. Member states are assumed to follow their own, clearly defined monolithic interests. The individualistic conception is discarded unceremoniously. There is no question about identification of *the* interest of each member state and no question about how the preferences of individual citizens are related to the "proper" role for an international organization. This has been a useful simplification and, as was elaborated above, has yielded important insights. But it is a major thesis of this work that further, and perhaps contrary conclusions can be reached by extending the individualist postulate to its logical limits. This approach accepts the idea that the preferences of individual citizens regarding the functions of an international organization are the ultimate inputs and that the optimal role for the organization can be derived efficiently from those individual preferences. Here, as elsewhere, some individuals may wish to seek advice or to delegate authority, whereas others may wish to express their preferences more directly.

The present work takes as axiomatic that the individual citizens' preferences serve as the ultimate inputs and asks how the alternative mechanisms for aggregating those preferences filter them and help to shape the institution and its functions. It emphasizes the rights and responsibilities of the individual in collective choices, including those about provision of globally shared goods.

The economic approach to assessing the appropriate role for international organizations focuses attention on the existence of goods that may plausibly be regarded as collective at the world level, that is, have properties that make efficient the sharing of their benefits and their costs among essentially all members of the world community. Concepts, principles, and procedures relevant to understanding optimal allocation to goods collective at lower levels of jurisdiction may provide useful insights into optimal allocation to global collective goods and hence make an important contribution to rational choice of functions for the international organization.

The economic conception of a means for determining an optimal set of programs for the United Nations is not offered here as a completely independent alternative. But it seems clear beyond any reasonable doubt that the economic approach can add a highly significant dimension to understanding the optimal level of programs for an international organization.

3. POLITICAL FUNCTIONS FOR COLLECTIVE-GOOD INTERMEDIARIES?

It can hardly be denied that the economic approach leaves unresolved very important questions that perhaps can be handled best in political terms. How, for example, are the officials of an international organization to be chosen? What division of responsibility can be adopted for submitting initiatives of the organization for evaluation by the individual members of the community? In more concrete terms and in the context of the existing entities, what might be the duties, responsibilities, and privileges of the Secretariat, the General Assembly, and the Security Council? [6]

Even if the officials of the international organization accept a strictly limited role in economic choices vis-à-vis the individual citizens, there will remain considerable scope for such political activities as bargaining, compromise, and voting on the programs to be presented to the community for its appraisal. The number of possible programs is, of course, indefinitely large. The practical duty of a strictly neutral international executive would be to process information about the community's evaluation of alternative programs and to generate estimates regarding the corresponding costs, to act as a collective-good intermediary, so to speak. Clearly, the "simple" processing of relevant information could be in itself a very considerable task. Expedients for considering limiting the range of alternatives would have to be adopted to avoid swamping the intermediary.[7] Experience and judgment would play a vital part in attempting to adjust programs toward the optimal level, and therefore the choice of individuals to serve in the intermediary mechanism and its internal organization are issues of vital concern. But the experience and judgment would be directed toward finding programs optimal from the viewpoint of the community as a whole. Consequently, the role described here is quite different from that currently associated with international organizational officials, who are expected to exercise their own judgment about the benefits and costs of the organization's activities. But even the initiation and adjustment of programs in conformance with community perception of net benefits would be a difficult, highly demanding task. The responsibility for initiation or formulation of programs would be very great. Those selected for community appraisal from among the large number of potential alternatives would have an important influence on the character of the ones actually adopted. Some individuals would wish to see the results of support levels for activities other than those suggested by the IO (international organization) officials. They may attempt by various means to initiate or otherwise to influence the intermediary's choice of programs for presentation to the citizenry. Thus, even where the organizational officer's role is defined strictly as collective-good intermediation, issues purely political in essence seem very likely to remain vital.

Given the importance of collective-good intermediation and the political issues it would raise, responsibility may be divided among separate sets of officials similar to those commonly observed at national and other levels of social organization. The scope for persuasion, bargaining, and compromise, that is, for political activity within and among these sets of officials quite clearly would remain large. The selection of individuals to serve as collective-good intermediaries also would remain an issue of considerable moment.

Furthermore, members of the community may wish to delegate responsibility beyond strictly collective-good intermediation. Indeed, almost inevitably the organization's officers will be far better informed than the average individual about the character, cost, and effects of various programs. Being more knowledgeable, their opinions about the benefits from alternative potential programs may exert, therefore, a considerable influence on the perception of the individual members of the community. In this sense, also, a "political" role for the international officials seems destined to remain prominent.

But the purely political aspects of the problem are beyond the scope of the current analysis. For simplification, to make our own problem manageable, we shall focus only on the implications of viewing the organization's officers as strictly providing the service of collective-good intermediation. We shall argue that this role may be extremely important if not dominant, leaving for later the appropriate qualifications and modifications.

Thus, it is not the purpose of this work to analyze in depth the internal organization of the global collective-good intermediary or the responsibilities of the various branches of the international organization in financial matters.[8] The purpose is to analyze the relationship between the organization, whatever its internal characteristics, and its constituents, individual human beings who are the ultimate beneficiaries of the organization's programs and the ultimate bearers of its costs. This is not, of course, to deny that there may be important relationships between the internal mechanisms of the organization and the efficiency of implementation of individual priorities but simply to argue that the mechanism for communication between "authorities" and constituents also may be extremely important for efficient choices relevant to global collective goods.

4. INDIVIDUALS, MEMBER STATES, AND FUNCTIONS OF INTERNATIONAL ORGANIZATIONS

A final and fundamental difference in the implications of individuals' as opposed to the member states' primacy in determining a role for international organization remains to be explored. A fairly convincing case can be made that the traditional conception seems in contradiction with the essential reason for creating the United Nations, namely to influence the behavior of those whose decisions lead to excessively costly disorder in the conduct of international affairs. When the prerogatives of "member states" for determing the scope of the United Nations activities are taken as fundamental, it is tantamount to accepting a minimal, or near minimal, role for the organization. The irrationality of national authorities' decisions to pursue violent conflict and preparations for it may be readily perceived by the remainder of the community, but the strict adherence to the inviolability of the "will of member states" leads inexorably to the interpretation that the international organizational role must be limited to minimal (if expanding) consensus. In other words, the international organizational programs will be limited to the minimum acceptable to the set of individuals at any given moment preferring the smallest role for the organization. Where there are national officials willing to employ violence to achieve their ends, *their* preferences become the extent of the minimal consensus. Then when their passions subside and others rise, it is again those individuals newly committed to disorder who define a similarly low limit to minimal consensus. It is as if the few individuals leaning toward use of violence during any given time period in a local community were taking turns perpetuating a veto of collective programs for maintaining order. Consequently, the shifting minority condoning disorder successively imposes its preferences on the remainder of the citizenry. Thus, a rotating minority not only may find no advantage in making its own contributions to support programs for orderly pursuit of justice but, in addition, may find advantage in preventing the support of the rest of the community.

The individualist approach is more in harmony with the view that specifically because on occasion "member states" (more precisely, national leaderships) become irrationally disorderly in their relations with one another the United Nations was created. The organization's fundamental mission is to reduce the cost of violence in world affairs that has been widely recognized as so great. Thus, the charge of the United Nations is not merely to reflect passively the views of all "member states" but to modify the admittedly irrational decisions taken in the "interest" of a particular state. In this view, the United Nations is conceived, not as a creature of, by, and for the individuals representing "member states," but as a means for constraining their behavior when they take, or appear poised to take decisions that the remainder of the individuals in the community regard as irrational.[9] Thus, the collective good to be provided by an international organization may be regarded as services to influence the behavior of specific members of the community at particular times.

Just as the activities of conflict controllers at the local level have negative "benefits" for some citizens who desire no restrictions on their pursuits, so in international affairs during certain periods some individuals will desire to be free of community representatives urging and working toward restraint in resort to threats and violence.[10]

From the individualist vantage point, programs with the purpose of influencing the choices of particular sets of national decision makers may constitute a collective good for which substantial support may be found among individual members of the world community, including perhaps many persons within potential adversary states.[11] A revealed evaluation of the benefits of international conflict control activities for a given distribution of individual preferences seems very likely to be a function also of the mechanism for revelation. Let us consider a mechanism that delegates the choice to the very sets of individuals whose behavior is to be modified, whose discretion is to be restricted, whose preferences will be given lesser weight, whose modes of life may be substantially altered, and whose decision-making services may suffer a decline in demand. Such a mechanism contains notable incentives with clear consequences for the revelation of community demand for IOPOPJ. In this context, the hypothesis might be suggested that, other things equal, individuals holding positions in the national governmental establishments will tend to be less favorably disposed toward IOPOPJ than others. Furthermore, the closer to the peaks in the national foreign policymaking apparatus, the greater may be the reluctance to expand IOPOPJ. The essential point is that the fundamental reason for United Nations security programs is to control and modify the behavior and decisions of "states" or, more accurately, of the subset of individuals who occupy the relevant positions. Support of international organizational programs by national foreign policy decision makers would be tantamount to admission that their own behavior not only is less than optimal but may well impose substantial net costs on the rest of the community, an admission that representatives at any level are understandably, especially loath to make. Direct financial support by individuals for programs whose purpose was to modify national officials' decisions may be less distasteful to the latter than actively seeking outside help.

Thus, emphasis on responsibility and authority of national elites creates a clear conflict of interest. Individuals with primary input into the decision about the scope of IOPOPJ are likely to prefer arrangements that maintain their primacy in the decision process.

In sum, our major purpose in this chapter has been to argue that the financial problem of international organizations is not entirely or even predominantly political, as has been argued so convincingly previously. There is a highly important economic dimension to the problem, and careful attention to it can yield many important insights into the fundamental questions regarding the optimal role for the United Nations, for its officials, and indeed for any administrators of programs creating global benefits.

A purely political approach emphasizes an evolving role for the international organization by expanding the consensual basis among "member states." Opportunities can be explored for persuading reluctant national governmental decision makers that their welfare may be served best by more extensive international programs for collective goods. When such decision makers perceive their mutual need for such programs and develop confidence in the capability and intentions of international organizations to provide them without bias, their scope for useful service will have been commensurately expanded.

The persuasiveness of this line of thought may be readily acknowledged. Nevertheless, adoption of the individualist postulate and of the closely related collective-good-intermediary conception of international organization suggests the relevance of a different scope for community consensus and, therefore, of an alternative mechanism for its expansion. More direct participation of a much wider set of individual human beings rather than that of a minute subset with clear conflict of interest and a record of very limited results is envisaged. Wider, more direct participation may yield an apparent foundation for support of global goods quite different from that visible when authority is delegated to representatives of member states. Evidence presented in Chapter VII suggests that within the more inclusive set of all persons in the community a rather broad and intense latent consensus already may exist. A means for probing its limits might be found in a mechanism more accurately portraying and aggregating elemental individual values.

Thus, the individualist postulate clearly suggests a rather different approach to financing global goods. Hardly coincidentally, the postulate constitutes also a fundamental foundation for the general, orthodox Western economic theory of sharing public goods, that is, for our basic analytical framework, to which we now are ready to turn.

NOTES

1. J. G. Stoessinger et al., pp. 3-34, provide an excellent, thorough exposition.

2. Financial independence in this context means sources of revenue other than those decided upon by governments of member nations.

3. As we shall see in more detail below, this may be especially important where many private individuals perceive benefits from international organizational programs which many national representatives might be extremely reluctant to accept.

4. Buchanan and Tullock, pp. 11-15, and Musgrave (1969), pp. 55-56, 103-4, provide excellent discussions of the postulate.

5. We might wish to attempt to discover the implications of the individualist postulate for an international organizational fiscal constitution (see Buchanan and Tullock), but our current task is rather more modest: it is an attempt to see the implications of the individualistic approach for incremental improvements of the existing mechanism.

6. One might wish to explore a rule prohibiting participation of parties to conflict in deciding on appropriate levels for programs aimed specifically at ameliorating or controlling their conflict.

7. This would seem especially true initially. As programs developed, marginal adjustments to ongoing activities would predominate.

8. On these matters see J. David Singer.

9. It is, of course, entirely possible that representatives of states in their less agitated moments may be willing themselves to accept, in principle, services of arbitrators, mediators, or other specialists in conflict control to promote increased consistency in the rationality of their interactions with potential adversaries.

10. An important issue will be: What are the community preferences regarding employment of violence in pursuit of the ends of particular individuals or groups? National governmental decision makers claim to be prepared to use violence only for the highest ends of the whole group—in the "national interest":

in pursuit of order, honor, freedom, democracy, equity; and so on. It is beyond the scope of the present work to analyze costs and benefits of use of violence to such ends, including in a program proposed by an international-good intermediary and "approved" through the support of individual members of the community. IOPOPJ may or may not involve violence or threats thereof. Strategies for resolving, controlling, or ameliorating international conflict, that is, the substance of IOPOPJ, are entirely beyond the scope of the present work, which is limited strictly to exploring the state of individual preferences and with the implications of alternative mechanisms for aggregating them.

11. Professor Fusfeld has shown that the resort to centralized planning and allocation during war may stem from need for drastic measures to induce the sacrifices of the rank and file desired by the established authorities. As he writes, "the costlier the war, the more people can be expected to oppose it, and the shorter the period of enthusiasm on the part of supporters. One of the largely unrecorded chapters of history is the opposition that has prevailed in all nations to all wars, even when the patriotic response has seemed to be overwhelming" (pp. 785-86). As Professor Knorr puts it, "Beyond doubt many ruling groups have traditionally taken a special interest in foreign and military policy as a means to the enjoyment of expected benefits to themselves, and have imposed the costs on their societies" (p. 41).

CHAPTER III

Economic Principles and Global Sharing

By almost any standard the general economic theory of sharing has advanced unusually rapidly in recent decades, and consequently it promises crucial perspectives on the global variety. As Professor James Buchanan has so aptly warned, however, relevant theories remain "in a preparadigm stage of development . . . no single treatment or presentation is likely to command universal assent among informed scholars nor is it likely to be free of its own ambiguities, confusions, and contradictions" (p. 202). There is no need for present purposes to review exhaustively the pertinent literature, much less to attempt to remove any of the ambiguities, confusions, or contradictions. We propose rather to draw upon basic concepts and principles for aid in analyzing alternative mechanisms, previously employed or proposed for global sharing.

Specifically, characteristics of goods virtually necessitating sharing, if they are produced at all, have been clearly identified. Guidelines for determining an efficient allocation of productive resources to public purposes have been elaborated. Problems associated with alternative institutional strategies for organizing creation of collective goods have been thoroughly explored. Let us consider each of these points in turn.

A. Characteristics of Collective Goods

Theorists agree that certain physical and economic characteristics of goods have an important bearing on whether, and to what extent, individuals will find sharing them efficient.[1] Properties generally accepted as necessitating sharing include nonexhaustiveness and nonexcludability. Nonexhaustiveness means that the good's contribution to satisfying the needs of any one individual in no way reduces its capacity to meet those of any other. Thus, the total produced is available to meet the needs of each and every member of the community. Nonexcludability means that once a good has been produced the cost of excluding anyone from enjoying its benefits is prohibitive.

Economists claim that important real goods possess characteristics closely approximating the pure theoretical concepts. Consider, for example, basic scholarly research resulting in a fundamental improvement in understanding that becomes common property of all. Possession of such understanding by any one individual or group in no way reduces its availability to any other person. Thus, the fruits of basic research appear to be characterized by an essentially pure nonexhaustiveness. Likewise, once such information becomes "common knowledge" available in standard references, elementary texts, and so on the costs of excluding anyone from its benefits becomes prohibitive, that is, it is a good with the property of nonexcludability.

B. Definition of an Optimum

Having determined that sharing a good is appropriate and perhaps even necessary, can we make any suggestions about how much of it to produce? If efficiency is the goal, contemporary orthodox theory suggests a plausible and persuasive although rather abstract guideline. Add the dollar values of all individual benefits associated with creation of each potential quantity of output. Determine how costs of production depend upon the quantity produced. Compare these sums of benefits with the associated costs of production. At the optimal output, the increment to the sum of benefits per unit increase in availability of the good must just balance the corresponding increment in costs.[2]

If, as neoclassical principles state, personal incremental benefit schedules coincide with corresponding personal demand schedules, the optimum may alternatively be indicated by the intersection of *their* vertical sum with the incremental cost schedule.

It is important to emphasize two points in this regard. First, such individual demand schedules for public goods differ significantly from ordinary demand schedules for purely private goods in that they are merely latent. That is, they reflect underlying desires that, in the absence of special institutions, individuals will have no material incentives to express. Second, the optimum is associated with only one point on the vertical sum of latent demands, namely, its intersection with the incremental cost schedule. Thus, it will be of crucial importance always to distinguish carefully between merely latent demands and demands that actually are disclosed.

In theory, evaluating costs presents no abnormal problems. The alternative uses of productive resources provide a measure of the costs of production whether they are employed in creating a private or a collective good. The men and equipment engaged in a peacekeeping program, for instance, can be costed in exactly the same fashion as those engaged in producing automobiles.

C. Difficulties in Attaining an Optimum

1. TRANSACTIONS COSTS

By contrast, evaluating benefits derived from collective goods is beset by special difficulties. In the first place, the costs of arranging a satisfactory contract are comparatively high simply because of the large number of persons who must be party to the agreement. They all must participate somehow in deciding how much to purchase and, simultaneously, how to share the cost. The number of relevant channels for communication rises exponentially with the number of participants, and consequently transactions costs quickly may become prohibitive. Special arrangements for communications almost always will be necessary to achieve a contract for anything approaching an optimal level of collective activity.

The costs of negotiating a contract can be greatly reduced by designating an *intermediary* to collect information about all the individual benefits and to represent potential consumers vis-à-vis potential producers. The lines of communication can focus on the intermediary rather than creating a vast impenetrable maze. But even if the intermediary could simply collect and add candidly stated estimates of individual benefits, the sheer volume of essential communications guarantees that his task will be formidable.

Nevertheless, a large volume of collective-good intermediation is, in fact, accomplished, most prominently by governments at various levels.[3] By one means or another officials estimate the potential benefits to their constituents from creating collective goods. They negotiate with potential providers, consummate contracts, and allocate cost shares among the members of the community. These are precisely the activities which from an economic viewpoint may be described as collective-good intermediation.

2. EVALUATING BENEFITS

Unfortunately, problems faced by a collective-good intermediary include more than simply adding a huge number of candidly stated individual benefits. According to orthodox principles, no individual who contemplates sharing a collective good with a large number of others has an incentive to reveal any indication of its worth to him. No matter how low the value he reports, he will enjoy full benefits from the quantity ultimately decided upon. Each person, in order to avoid providing a basis for an assessment in proportion to the benefit he discloses, may perceive an advantage in claiming the good is worth nothing to him. If he believes that the other members of the group will pay for it, he need contribute nothing, with no appreciable effect on its availability. Furthermore, the free rider may conclude that he is not imposing significantly on society and, inasmuch as the costs of his nonparticipation are distributed equally over the remainder of the individuals in the community, none would, in fact, be perceptibly affected. If he believes, on the other hand, that others will contribute a total insufficient to pay for the collective good, he would only lose by supporting a lost cause, so to speak. Thus, Buchanan argues, "regardless of how the individual estimates the behavior of others, he must always rationally choose the free rider alternative. Since all individuals will tend to act similarly, the facility [collective good] will not be constructed [produced] from proceeds of wholly voluntary contributions" (p. 89).[4] This clearly is a very strong statement and apparently is refuted by the fact that we do observe private arrangements for providing at least some public goods.

The strong hypothesis may be distinguished from a "weak" version frequently encountered in the literature. Whereas the strong version goes so far as to claim that *no* benefits will be acknowledged, the weaker one states that each individual will have good reason to understate his benefit and that consequently production, while possibly positive, will be less than optimal.

It must be emphasized that the weak free rider hypothesis is consistent with at least some voluntarily arranged output of public goods. Individuals with very intense desires may contribute voluntarily to the provision of certain goods. Others with positive desires, though less intense, won't, with underprovision the consequence. Many institutions that emerge as public good intermediaries operate with purely voluntary contributions but apparently at less than the optimal level.

Under a completely voluntary regime, the strength or weakness of proclivities toward free riding will essentially govern the extent to which an optimal allocation will be approached. Measurement of such proclivities in any systematic way is in very early stages of development, and lack of a solid empirical foundation remains a major source of uncertainty in predicting the consequences of adopting alternative institutions.

True, various attempts to relate the free rider hypothesis to empirical evidence have been reported. Professor Mancur Olson has collected a considerable amount of anecdotal evidence that he interprets as strongly supporting it. Professors Martin and Anita Pfaff, on the other hand, cite surveys suggesting that in certain communities large percentages of taxpayers have regarded their payments as essentially voluntary (p. 295). Professor Peter Bohm (1971) has pointed out that potential consumers seem to reveal preferences quite clearly through political parties, pressure groups, and opinion polls.

In the mid-1970s Americans, in addition to paying several hundred billion dollars in taxes have contributed each year roughly $25 billion or about 2 percent of GNP for a variety of collective purposes (U.S. Bureau of the Census, p. 299). Furthermore, contributions in kind, not subject to tax, undoubtedly also amounted to many billions of dollars.[5] Many questions might be raised pertinent to the meaning of this apparently quite substantial revelation of demand. Do these data reflect reports of recipients or of contributors? To what extent were the apparent sacrifices associated with financial contributions mitigated by deductions from taxable income? Were the demands revealed in large- or small-group environments? Thorough investigations to provide answers will greatly enhance our understanding of sharing behavior.

The results of several experiments directed toward testing the free rider hypothesis have been published.[6] Their purposes have been quite limited, and conclusions remain tentative, but the general approach, if refined and expanded, promises to provide a useful beginning toward the empirical foundation we need. In the current state of knowledge we can conclude that a regime of purely voluntary exchange doubtlessly would be vulnerable to some free riding. However, we also can hardly rule out the possibility of financing significant levels of collective activity through essentially voluntary contributions.

Can institutions be devised that avoid the inefficiencies stemming from free riding without creating undesired side effects? The most prominent approach suggests adopting taxes along with voting decision rules for approving or rejecting expenditure proposals. Given an unavoidable tax obligation and provided an opportunity to choose between expenditures on alternative collective goods, individuals can advance their own welfare by voting for programs they prefer, thereby revealing their preferences, at least in some degree. Unfortunately, neither can efficiency be attained nor can all other problems be eliminated simply by government intervention.

The potential consequences of a great variety of tax-voting mechanisms have been very thoroughly explored, [7] but none has proven flawless, even in theory. With few exceptions, they have tended to create the possibility of "forced rides," that is, tax obligations for some persons in excess of benefits they receive while simultaneously providing a windfall gain for others. A unanimity decision rule is one exception, but it clearly limits very severely the scope for collective action.[8]

"Demand-revealing" mechanisms [9] also promise to avoid both free- and forced-riding. But they are in very early stages of development. Although such mechanisms have already been tested experimentally (Smith), significant problems will have to be overcome before successful everyday applications can be anticipated.

In practice, of course, taxes have been employed along with representation and, frequently, simple majority voting rules, creating a potential for dissatisfied minorities, whether because of forced rides or because of rejected programs.

Thus, the rational individual contemplating adoption of collective-good decision rules faces a strategic dilemma, a trade-off between creating a potential for free rides on the one hand and for forced rides on the other. Explicit recognition of this dilemma presumably will promote rational selection of a mechanism well suited to attaining social objectives.

3. INITIATING INTERMEDIATION

Still another general problem associated with sharing, but with special relevance at the global level, is the difficulty of initiating intermediation. Suppose that aside from the absence of an intermediary conditions are propitious for creation of a collective good. Specifically, suppose the sum of *potential* individual benefits exceeds the *potential* cost of production. But in the absence of an intermediary, aggregation of individual benefits is ineffective if not impossible. Without such an aggregation, the costs of the collective good, including remuneration of the intermediary, cannot be covered, and consequently the intermediary cannot exist. How can the vicious circle be broken?

In brief, breaking the vicious circle requires the activity of collective-good innovators who are willing to sacrifice a portion of their wealth voluntarily, without a commitment of support from all of the members of the community. Thus, as Professor Burton Weisbrod has suggested, provision for collective goods by voluntary organization of relatively small groups may be expected to precede broader support through government (p. 23). Weisbrod cites the funds donated by private philanthropy in sixteenth-century England for "schools, hospitals, roads (nontoll), fire fighting apparatus, public parks, bridges, dikes and causeways, digging of drainage canals, waterworks, wharves and docks, harbor cleaning, libraries, care of prisoners in jails, and charity to the poor—in short, for the gamut of non-military goods that we identify today as governmental responsibilities." The initial contributors to a pure collective good may be able to gain some of its net benefits while simultaneously attempting to demonstrate them to others in the community and to enlist their support. Professors Lance Davis and Douglas North have elaborated a very interesting theory of institutional innovation that attempts to predict "the length of time that passes between the recognition of . . . potential profit and the emergence of the new arrangement" (p. 39). They have provided numerous accounts of episodes from American history relevant to innovation of arrangements for sharing. In their scheme, an important role is played by "primary action groups" (p. 8) who recognize the potential for raising net income through institutional innovations often involving creation of collective goods.

In conclusion, nonexhaustiveness, nonexcludability, the role of individual benefits in defining an optimal allocation, the potential propensity for free riding, the danger of forced rides and of conflict and controversy promoted by them, the existence of large transactions costs, and the role of collective-good intermediation and innovation are all fundamental elements of a tool kit for would-be constructors of rational mechanisms for sharing. How can such tools be used in the specific context of understanding globally collective goods? They can aid in understanding the consequences of previously employed mechanisms.[10] They should be helpful also for deriving implications of alternative proposals. Let us consider then the traditional rationales guiding international cost-sharing decisions to see how.

NOTES

1. Steiner, Mishan, and Head may be consulted for more detailed discussions.

2. The relevance of the individualist postulate is very clear in this approach. The benefit received by each and every person is to be counted, and the social benefit is nothing more than the sum of all the personal benefits derived from existence of the good.

3. Collective-good intermediation may be characterized by natural monopoly. The costs of duplication and reconciliation if more than one organization participated may tend to be quite high.

4. Terms in brackets added.

5. The value of donated labor services (excluding volunteers for religious organizations) has been evaluated at $14 billion in 1964 (Wolozin, p. 208).

6. Detailed discussions may be found in Smith and the references cited there.

7. Professor Dennis Mueller has provided a very useful survey and guide to the pertinent literature.

8. Buchanan and Tullock provide the modern classic discussion of the costs that may accompany constitutional commitment to sharing.

9. See Bohm, Clarke, Groves and Ledyard, Smith, and Tideman and Tullock for examples.

10. At the same time, examination of existing arrangements and their consequences may provide some insights into the applicability of the principles themselves.

CHAPTER IV

Traditional Approaches to International Cost Sharing

Sharing benefits and costs internationally is by no means without precedent. By what principles, if any, has previous practice been guided? What problems have been encountered? How in fact have expenditures and cost shares been determined? Does the perspective provided by contemporary doctrine outlined in the preceding chapter suggest means for avoiding difficulties apparently associated with the traditional approaches? Let us see.

A. Ability to Pay or Benefit

Formulas adopted by the League of Nations, the United Nations, their affiliates, and other such organizations faced with the problem of allocating cost shares often have been defended on the basis of presumed benefit or of ability to pay, the traditional guidelines for equity in public expenditure and tax policy. Very succinctly, the benefit doctrine states that each participant in a sharing arrangement should pay in proportion to the value of the collective good to him. Where international sharing takes place, costs should be allocated in proportion to the value perceived by citizens of the nations that are parties to the agreement. From this perspective, the benefit created is determined by satisfactions subjec-

31

tively evaluated by individual human beings, and they should support creation of the good exactly in proportion.

The ability-to-pay argument emphasizes that whatever the level of expenditure, and however it is decided, cost shares should be allocated according to ability to pay. The close association of this doctrine with the organic conception of social needs is readily apparent. Costs are incurred for general social purposes and constitute, therefore, an obligation of society. This obligation should be distributed among individuals of the social unit in a fashion imposing the least sacrifice. And the least sacrifice results when cost shares are assigned according to ability to pay.

The benefit doctrine accords more closely with the modern economic definition of an efficient allocation. As we have seen in Chapter III, the aggregation of individual benefits plays a vital role in determining an efficient level of output. The ability-to-pay doctrine provides no guidance regarding the extent to which resources might profitably be allocated to a collective program.

B. Difficulties in Implementation

Neither of the approaches can be implemented without considerable difficulty, and the difficulties never are more formidable than when global sharing is at issue. The benefit criterion, although theoretically attractive, requires an enormous amount of information from individuals. Indeed, benefit as an explicit, operational criterion for international sharing has been rejected outright on the basis of insurmountable costs of obtaining requisite data (Schelling, p. 466).[1] Thus, almost by default, where general principles pertinent to international cost sharing have been sought, attention has been focused on ability to pay.[2] An examination of its advantages and disadvantages in somewhat more detail therefore seems necessary at this point.

1. ABILITY TO PAY

On some accounts focus on ability to pay may seem promising. Apparently, necessary information has become much more readily available, accurate, and reliable. Extensive data on personal incomes are collected by national governments for tax purposes. National income accounting has been extensively developed theoretically and has been much more widely applied. Standard accounts to facilitate international comparisons have been established. All this has, of course, facilitated use of income statistics as a measure of ability to contribute to international organizations. But on further consideration the remaining difficulties stand out more prominently.

First of all, annual income is hardly a unique indicator of ability to pay. Wealth, consumption, liquidity, leisure,[3] and so on may be proposed in its stead. A virtually endless list of objections to material income in any given year could be raised. It can be a starting point, perhaps, but little more.

a. Concept. The mere definition of income constitutes a formidable problem even for an individual, let alone a large group. Conceptions vary from time to time and from place to place. Development and implementation of national accounting has been uneven and diverse. At best, it is a very complex activity requiring highly debatable decisions at many points. Even the most refined of national accounting statistics can hardly be regarded as anything more than the crudest of first approximations to variations in the ability to pay, and extra obstacles must be surmounted when using income as a criterion in the international context.

b. Conversion. Conversion of various national income estimates into a common denomination involves very serious difficulties. The rates at which national currencies exchange, whether set officially or through market forces, frequently do not reflect accurately the domestic purchasing power of a currency. Milton Gilbert and his associates have shown, for example, that the national incomes of certain European countries in the 1950s were understated by more than 33 percent compared with the United States when exchange rates rather than more accurate purchasing power parities were used for the conversion to a common currency (p. 165).

c. Index number problem. Even if all countries adopted a uniform procedure so that all the difficult decisions about scope, prices, taxes, subsidies, and so on were identical, and even if perfectly accurate purchasing power parities were found, index number ambiguity would remain, and it alone could create an essentially insuperable problem for obtaining a precise and unique answer to the comparative size of national incomes. That is, the relative size of any two countries' national incomes still may depend heavily upon the currency in which the comparison is made. If, for example, we attempt to compare Soviet and American abilities to contribute to a joint program, we may wish to compare the size of their respective national incomes measured either in rubles or in dollars. If so, we will find that the relative size, and therefore indicated ability to pay, will depend heavily upon an arbitrary choice of currency. Specifically, we have good reason to suspect that the national income of the USSR will be smaller in comparison with that in the

United States when rubles rather than dollars are used as the common currency. The reason is basically a negative correlation between relative prices and relative availability of goods in both countries. In other words, items with lower prices tend to be associated with greater amounts within a country. Thus, goods priced relatively lower in the United States are usually those that are comparatively more abundantly available there. Consequently, when the two (national) sets of real goods and services are valued at American prices, a larger weight is accorded those items that are relatively more abundantly available than if Soviet values were used. Similarly, when the two sets of goods are aggregated with Soviet prices, a heavier weight is accorded to items relatively more abundant in the United States. In sum, when a country's physical outputs are added up with another's monetary unit as the common denominator, the result is to apply relatively high prices to comparatively large quantities and relatively low prices to comparatively small quantities. Thus, the relative size of a country's national income will be greater when the other country's unit prices are applied to both national sets of real goods and services.

These relationships have been verified repeatedly in various empirical investigations involving international and intertemporal comparisons of national income accounting aggregates, and the ambiguities often are substantial. To cite another very important example, Abram Bergson has shown that in 1965 Soviet gross national product was 35 percent of that in the United States when measured in rubles but 57.5 percent of that in the United States, that is, almost 65 percent higher, when measured in U.S. prices. Thus, as a practical matter the ability to pay of the countries with by far the largest GNPs can be measured only with an enormous margin of ambiguity from this one source alone.[4]

d. Adjustments to income. Adjustments to income sometimes have been advocated as necessary to arive at more accurate estimates of ability to pay. Bargainers in cost-sharing negotiations have argued that temporary deviations from normal economic conditions: destruction from war, floods, or storms; an influx of refugees; and so on constitute sufficient grounds for special treatment. Such pleas seem to be refuted effectively, however, by showing that special circumstances often are already reflected in the national income accounts, so that any further adjustment would constitute, in effect, double counting. Temporary deviations from "normal" can be compensated for by making the average over several years the indicator of ability to pay.

Gold outflows or deficits in the balance of payments occasionally have been cited as evidence of inability to contribute. Presumably a deficit eventually will require some sort of adjustment. But the country's share in financing international projects is hardly a residual claimant on resources that should or, in all probability could, allow the adjustment. As a practical matter contributions to international programs often may be small relative to international payments deficits. In any event, efficiency may require the allocation to the global good on the basis of benefit and/or ability, and an adjustment elsewhere, presumably a reduction in the price of the country's currency. The position that no systematic allowances for foreign exchange difficulties should be made seems sound from the standpoint of efficiency.

e. Specification of schedule. Acceptance of the ability-to-pay principle leaves open the question of specification of the exact numerical schedule. Again difficulties are compounded when international sharing is concerned. If progressivity in shares is agreed upon, should it be with reference to national average per capita incomes or to individual incomes? If the criterion is national averages, high-income residents of low-income countries will not be assessed as much as persons with the identical incomes residing in high-income countries. If the criterion is personal income, the difficulty of administration will be greatly increased. In early stages of development of international organization the need for costly information on individual incomes can be avoided by stating ability-to-pay principles with reference to national averages. But from a wider and longer-term perspective, efficiency and equity would be better served by focusing rather upon individuals.

The picture is further muddled by the fact that strictly proportional sharing on the basis of national per capita incomes may tend to result in progressivity in sharing in real terms. If, as is often thought, observed exchange rates overstate the real purchasing power of money in more affluent nations, their real relative incomes are lower than suggested by simple comparisons of money incomes.[5] Thus, a schedule of shares progressive in money terms in fact will be even more steeply progressive in real terms.

f. Contributions in kind. Certain problems are associated with the fact that international support of joint programs often takes the form of contributions in kind. National contingents of manpower and equipment may participate directly in provision of an international collective good; peacekeeping services, for example. In many countries recruits are under compulsion to serve and receive little compensation beyond food, clothing, medical care, and so on—with the total amounting to rather less than their civilian opportunity costs. In others they receive in addition monetary allowances and privileges that bring their compensation to a total also rather less than their civilian opportunity costs. In still others monetary allowances and privileges along with income-in-kind approach much more closely their best civilian alternative, and consequently international incomparabilities arise. Various approaches to improving the accuracy of comparative contributions of military manpower may be envisaged. One might attempt to compare the "productivity" of soldiers from various nations, but clearly that is not likely to prove fruitful. All soldiers regardless of nationality may be valued at the average remuneration (monetary and in kind) of all the sharing countries. Finally, the soldiers may be valued according to their respective domestic opportunity costs. The latter procedure would in all probability be consistent with that used in valuing other contributed inputs such as materials or equipment.

g. Potential procedures. These, then, are some of the inevitable problems encountered when focusing on an ability-to-pay approach to cost sharing. Is it possible to point to any procedures potentially facilitating international cost sharing, given focus on ability to pay? It would be difficult to defend a claim that we can do anything more than suggest a few tentative steps toward ad hoc rules of thumb. Ability to pay is indeed nothing more than a relevant variable. By itself it clearly does not constitute a well-defined model precisely linking objectives of equity and efficiency with available policy instruments. Thus, we have no complete model, let alone evidence to the effect that it reflects reality closely enough to inspire confidence that if only we adopt certain rules we can anticipate realization of objectives subject to a specifiable distribution of error.

By far the most prominent "principle," despite its extremely fragile theoretical base, sharing the costs of collective goods *in proportion* to material income, seems to command considerable attention and respect as, if nothing else, a convenient point of departure. It seems to have constituted a first approximation to a "prominent solution" to the cost-sharing problem.

Proportionality has the great virtue of simplicity, and simplicity takes on added significance where extraordinarily difficult international comparisons raise very serious doubts about the meaningfulness of virtually all components of any scheme likely to be adopted. It is true that proportionality implies that richer individuals will pay higher unit prices for the same item, but this of course is entirely consistent with the modern economic conception of efficiency, if the good is normal. There may also be some superficial plausibility to the notion that somehow sacrifices of equal percentages of income constitute an equal burden. Proportionality over a wide range is entirely compatible with the elements of progressivity that can be incorporated, also quite simply, by the device of exemptions.

Exemptions themselves have the added attraction that they deal with a strategic aspect of equity, the alleviation of poverty. Avoidance of inequities at the higher levels of income may generally be regarded as a positive goal, but their avoidance at lower levels may be more generally regarded as crucial.

2. CONCEPTUAL FLAW IN FOCUS ON CAPACITY

All told, despite the foothold provided by enormous progress in the theory and practice of international cost sharing, opportunities for improvement, "reserves," as the Russians say, remain enormous. The perspective provided by contemporary doctrine suggests that focus on the ability to pay in pursuit of equity has resulted in neglect of efficiency and in fact contains a fatal conceptual flaw. The essential point is that equity may be perceived as depending, not only on ability to pay, but also on the benefits accruing to the individual contributors. A set of cost shares that appears equitable on the basis of ability to pay may appear entirely inequitable to some when the distribution of benefits is taken into account. Sharing costs according to capacity consequently risks provoking controversey and determined resistance of those allocated cost shares entirely out of proportion to their evaluation of the good. This point is most salient when a potential sharer clearly perceives only negative consequences from a proposed program but may be hardly any less vital when he perceives a value quite small relative to his allocated cost. In such circumstances, attempts to achieve compromise formulas solely on the basis of ability to pay promise to be a difficult and unrewarding task often doomed to failure. The controversies over sharing UN peacekeeping expenses, reviewed in the following chapter, provide a dramatic example of difficulties inevitable when inadequate attention is paid to the distribution of benefits from a program. Even if we close eyes and ears to this monumental conceptual flaw and gratefully accept the guidance, such as it may be, that the ability-to-pay criterion may provide, we can hardly hope for anything but the grossest sort of approximation to an optimal solution. The contemporary consensus indicator of ability to pay—income—can serve at the very best as only a crude measure, and hardly a precise and reliable guide to equity. Index number ambiguity alone presents a formidable obstacle. Disparities in economic ideology and concepts, national income accounting procedures and efforts, as well as in foreign exchange rates and internal purchasing power parities compound the problem.

3. "RELEVANT CONSIDERATIONS"

When in the mid-1950s Thomas Schelling surveyed prospective developments in international cost sharing, he foresaw that further analysis would emphasize "relevant considerations" rather than precise and objective formulas. Relevant considerations can be many and may include, along with the more traditional concepts and principles, notions related to conflict, bargaining, and strategy. Thus, collaboration, concessions, goodwill, and trust may be very useful concepts when attempting to understand the outcome of a specific global cost-sharing negotiation. Goodwill and trust may be valuable commodities attainable through concessions and collaboration and rationally purchased at some temporary sacrifice of material goods and services. A spirit of accommodation and cooperation may be more conducive to promoting the welfare of all concerned from a longer-term perspective than strict adherence to attempts at exacting the last half milligram of selfish advantage in the short run. These notions are likely to be especially important from a dynamic point of view, since the actions and decisions of the parties may interact to affect mutually their outlook, preferences, and hence bargaining positions in subsequent periods.

For a number of reasons the prospects for notable improvements facilitating rational agreements for obtaining the benefits and sharing the costs of international programs seem much brighter than only a few decades ago. Modern principles suggest that a "relevant consideration" with eminently great promise and deserving of much more attention in the future is the distribution of benefits among the cost-sharing groups and probably even among individual human beings. The theoretical relevance of benefits has long been recognized, of course, and stress on ability to pay has stemmed from the conviction that their evaluation is infeasible. Within the foreseeable future, however, much more accurate and reliable estimation of total benefits and their distribution in the global community may be possible. This possibility is founded on the potential for eliciting *economic* evaluations of global goods by individual human beings and on the technical advance in the collection and analysis of data.

Another relevant consideration in this context is concern for the sovereignty, so to say, of individual human beings, who might retain the right to make their own evaluation of the worth of global goods. Emphasis on individual sovereignty risks, of course, the abuse by free riders who in fact value global goods highly but dissemble to gain some selfish advantage. At present, however, there seems much solider reason than formerly to suspect that conditions can be created that will lead to useful revelations of willingness to contribute to collective goods generally. In any event, individual sovereignty would have the considerable advantage of avoiding the compulsion that almost inevitably would violate the sense of justice and equity of those individuals who, although compelled to contribute, genuinely valued the benefits of global programs very little or not at all. Much more evidence will be needed on willingness, or unwillingness, to disclose evaluations of collective goods before a confident judgment can be made as to whether the amount of free-riding would suffice to offset the substantial advantages that a mechanism emphasizing greater individual participation may offer.

Still another relevant consideration is the shifting emphasis among objectives. In the past, concern has centered on equity and fair shares, but in the future efficiency almost certainly will be more heavily stressed. The point is not that equity is any less important than previously but that attainment of a generally accepted definition seems as remote and elusive as ever.

No attempt can be made here to review accumulated wisdom pertinent to concepts of equity, but a plethora of deep-seated, long-standing, and probably contradictory convictions surely is involved. Equity remains ill defined with almost as many conceptions as conceivers, a notion fully as elusive in the context of global sharing as in others. It involves individual values that seem bound to entail numerous conflicts, resolvable only through compromise, accommodation, and sensitivity to the attitudes of others. With the objective so ill defined, an attempt at formulating principles to guide its attainment seems doomed at the outset.

The fixation on equity has constituted an implicit, though probably unintended disavowal of efficiency, with distinctly detrimental results. The quest for the grail of equity based on ability to pay has distracted attention from efficiency that under current conditions may be more readily attainable and might compensate at least in part for perceived inadequacies on the equity front.

All this is in no way intended as a simple advocacy of a particular set of values. The point is rather that large potential gains may be available from improved efficiency simply because it is better understood and therefore perhaps more readily attainable in the near term.

Furthermore, if placed in the perspective of the overall distribution of income and wealth, it is clear that justice in sharing costs of global goods simply is not a severe problem. At foreseeable levels of provision of global goods, attainment of fair shares would make only a minor contribution to solving the problem of deprivation and poverty, let alone the general issue of equity.

A possible exception to the theme of the preceding paragraph seems worth noting here. That is, global transfers of income and wealth themselves seem to have the properties of collective goods and may claim substantial contributions in an efficient global allocation. An indirect means for accomplishing such transfers would be, of course, universal sharing of the benefits of global goods, such as programs for order in the pursuit of justice, while exempting the poor from shares in the cost.

This indirect method of redistribution is subject, nevertheless, to at least two serious objections. However necessary most global goods other than income transfers might be for the world's deprived, their provision in efficient quantities probably would not suffice to eliminate poverty. Undoubtedly some direct transfers and development aid will be needed. Second, indirect redistribution constitutes a form of transfer in kind of the sort so widely recognized as blatantly inefficient. Perhaps the more efficient procedure would be first to decide the issue of income transfers and then to allow global goods to compete with all others for the monetary ballots of all members of the community. Some among the poorest will find global goods sufficiently attractive to warrant some small (in absolute terms) sacrifice of other items.

In sum, although equity in global cost sharing will remain an attractive goal, the gains from greater focus on efficiency under circumstances likely to prevail in the foreseeable future appear to be much more easily attainable. If, as seems virtually certain, there have been substantial underallocations of resources to global collective goods,[6] correspondingly substantial potential gains in output are implied. Indeed, inasmuch as many important preconditions already seem to have been achieved, such gains in output may be comparatively easily available and with no especially compelling reason to expect that they need to be purchased at the expense of extensive violations of individual perceptions of equity. Whereas care to avoid gross violations of perceptions of equity remains worthwhile, improved efficiency may be the predominant source of potential gain during the next several decades.

Since parts of the foregoing argument may be perceived as utopian, it might be well to recall that important global collective programs have already accomplished a great deal while operating under individual sovereignty with the services of merely embryonic collective-good intermediaries. The potential for sharing global goods promising very large aggregate benefits to members of the world community remains largely unexplored.

By no means should these embryonic efforts be belittled. The very existence of international organizations that can serve as collective-good intermediaries represents an enormously important foundation for futher rationalization of global cost and benefit sharing. They have established reputations for organizing programs and facilities, and they constitute a vital foundation for erecting the communications mechanisms needed for obtaining individual evaluations of global goods.

Finally, emphasis on efficiency, benefits, and individual sovereignty seems especially promising at the present time because of the well-known general progress in the performance of technical tasks such as designing sample surveys, drawing inferences, storing and processing data, and so on. Rational choices regarding global goods clearly will require substantial informational inputs, and these in turn will be greatly facilitated by modern means of transmitting and analyzing data.

In sum, advances in the theory of sharing; existence of potential collective-good intermediaries; and technical advances in data collection, transmission, and processing promise to enhance greatly the feasibility of stressing distribution of benefits from global goods among individuals in the world community, a vital ingredient for any attempt at approximating both the optimal allocation to collective goods and an "equitable" distribution of the burden.

C. United Nations Cost-sharing Practice—Procedures and Consequences

Having examined on a rather abstract level traditional principles, let us now turn to one of the more prominent examples of their application. International cost and benefit sharing has proceeded well beyond the merely speculative stage, even if one excludes the sharing implied by military alliances. As early as 1963 Kravis and Davenport reported that the U.S. government channeled financial support to more than seventy international organizations. True, many of their budgets were small by comparison with those of most national governments and even many private organizations, but some had attained substantial levels. Annual expenditures of the United Nations system [7] were on the order of $1 billion annually by the early 1970s (Elmandjra, pp. 232 ff.). Thus, global sharing already has attained such dimensions that the cost-allocation solutions adopted and the experience of participants in actual international organizations might contribute notably to understanding the general process.

The varieties of international cost-sharing experience are quite substantial. Each of the global organizations has had to face up to the issue, and many have responded with their own unique approach to sharing costs.

On the other hand, tradition and precedent have played important roles in formulating "fiscal constitutions," so to speak, of international organizations, so that mechanisms adopted have often been similar and sometimes identical. Furthermore, formally independent entities such as the UN's specialized agencies may nevertheless create fiscal institutions, policies, and procedures nearly identical with those of the parent organization.

The methods, mechanisms, or procedures adopted by each international organization reflect the outcome of discussion and debate among individuals to whom responsibility has been delegated. Mechanisms proposed in the course of debate but not adopted often also are interesting, to say the least. The motives of proposers may contribute to an understanding of why one particular mechanism rather than another is chosen and of the total situation in which a cost-sharing method is adopted. Thus, a summary of the debate, the positions advanced, and the compromises achieved might contribute to understanding the outcomes of specific cost-sharing negotiations.

It is nevertheless beyond the scope of the present work to attempt an extensive examination of individual positions on the appropriate arrangements for sharing costs of the United Nations organization, especially of their trends and interactions. Major participants in the debate simultaneously have been parties to conflicts, and consequently the debate reflects jockeying for position in specific circumstances by bitter, sometimes almost mortal adversaries as much or more than attempts at rational collaboration to share efficiently benefits and costs of collective goods. Consequently, attempts to distill essential, general truths from ideas expressed by negotiators defending particular special interests constitutes an especially difficult and probably unrewarding task. The emphasis here will be rather on elaboration of procedures actually adopted and an analysis of their consequences.

The United Nations surely is the foremost historical example of an attempt at performing the function of global collective-good intermediation, and it is clearly the number one candidate, whatever its current circumstances, for performing that function in the future. Its procedures, their development, and their consequences are, therefore, of most general interest.

The United Nations organization itself has been responsible for many and variegated programs. The mechanisms employed to obtain the financial wherewithal also have been diverse. For purposes of analysis, it will be convenient to consider separately the regular budget, peacekeeping operations, special voluntary programs, and those of the specialized agencies, since the arrangements within these categories are quite similar but differ considerably one from the other.

The regular budget includes appropriations for: sessions of the General Assembly and the councils; personnel; buildings and equipment; special expenses; technical programs; special missions and related activities; the Office of the United Nations High Commission for Refugees; and the International Court of Justice. Thus, the regular budget pertains largely to the conference and general administrative functions of the organization.

The Charter sets forth the strategy for determining the budget. According to it, the General Assembly is to be responsible for considering and approving the budget and apportioning expenses among the members. Pluralities of two thirds are required for passage of items relevant to the budget. A member in arrears loses voting privileges in the General Assembly when the amount past due equals or exceeds its assessments over the preceding two years.

Although final budgetary authority rests with the General Assembly, the executive branch of necessity becomes heavily involved in the process. Departmental estimates must be made, reviewed, collated, and prepared for presentation to the General Assembly. In practice, detailed examination of the budget also is the responsibility of the General Assembly's Advisory Committee on Administrative and Budgetary Questions. Thus, the General Assembly receives for consideration both the Secretariat's estimates and a report on them by the Advisory Committee.

Departmental estimates reflect, of course, requirements imposed on them by the programs and activities called for by the secretary general in response to the initiatives of the General Assembly. Thus the process is continuous and interrelated.

Logically, the determination of sources of funds and expenditures is inextricably connected, and as J. David Singer has stated, "During the various phases of the authorization, formulation, examination, and appropriation processes, the revenue problem is ever-present, often explicitly and always implicitly. Conversely, in the search for revenue, much emphasis is placed on the size and nature of the appropriations which have to be matched" (p. 122). Nevertheless, "needed" programs are approved with the problem of meeting the associated costs and deciding on their apportionment left for later consideration. Furthermore, although adoption of programs is accomplished with consideration of costs at least implicitly in the minds of decision makers, their distribution among the membership has been treated as an essentially separable problem. An administrative reflection of this fact is that the Committee on Contributions has drafted proposed scales of assessments with no references to the size of programs and their costs. Notice that the level of programs to be undertaken and the associated costs have not been regarded as subject to economic principles. These are issues to be decided upon by governmental representatives on the basis of judgments and compromise. The portion of the Charter dealing with economic issues pertains merely to the method for sharing costs among the membership, and even here in a very general way.

Numerical recommendations for assessments have been the responsibility of a Committee on Contributions under terms of reference and directives provided by the General Assembly.[8] The guidance of the General Assembly can be summarized as follows. Cost shares were to be determined by capacity to pay with comparative national income as the primary guide. Further factors to be considered included income per capita, temporary economic "dislocation" because of World War II, and availability of foreign currency. The General Assembly also has: (1) set in principle a progressively lower limit on the assessment of the highest contributor,[9] (2) requested that, in normal times, the per capita assessment of no member state should exceed the per capita assessment of the largest contributor; (3) requested lowering the limit on minimum contributions from 0.04 percent, effective from 1946 through 1972, to 0.02 percent; and (4) requested that special attention be given to the developing countries in view of their economic and financial problems.

The work of the Committee on Contributions can be illustrated with reference to its preparation of the scale of assessments for 1974-76. Data for the period 1969-71 were used as the foundation, and all national income figures were stated in terms of U.S. dollars. Problems arising from a variety of national policies regarding exchange rates were resolved as indicated in the tabulation.

TABLE 1 [a]

Environment	Procedure
A. Single fixed exchange rate under the Articles of Agreement of the International Monetary Fund (IMF)	Use fixed par value
B. Officially altered under IMF	Time-weighted average
C. No par value under IMF but single official fixed exchange rate and reasonable price stability	Official rate

D. Currencies "realigned" in 1971 without a formal devaluation or revaluation	Essentially monthly averages of the end-of-month effective rates as reported in *International Financial Statistics* of IMF
E. Multiple exchange rate systems with reasonable price stability	One rate chosen after consideration of relevant factors, such as "the relative importance of the rate of the external transactions of the country."
F. Multiple exchange rate systems with inflation	One rate chosen[b]
G. Multiple exchange rates	Weighted average
H. Prices did not bear a "reasonable" relationship to their respective exchange rates	National income estimates "were converted at 'adjusted exchange rates,' . . . obtained by adjusting some selected year's exchange rate, believed to represent a reasonable approximation to the purchasing power ratio of the two countries, by the ratio of relative price changes of the two countries since the base year."

or

When a national income series was available in constant prices of a year during which a reasonable exchange rate prevailed, estimates in constant prices for the period under review were converted at the exchange rate of the base year and were then adjusted to the current price basis by applying the change in the purchasing power of the U.S. dollar.

or

Estimates derived directly in U.S. dollars from production data.

---

[a] *Report of the Committee on Contributions to the General Assembly* (twenty-eighth session).

[b] Feasible since exchange rates were adjusted generally in proportion to the price level.

In view of its terms of reference, it is not surprising that the Committee on Contributions has not reduced its formula to a simple (or complex) mathematical statement. It still depends to a significant degree on "relevant considerations." Some of the most relevant are exchange rates and currency inflation.

Since 1964 the committee has compiled and consulted data on net national products at market prices for all member states as an effort toward achieving values more easily comparable with the data submitted by those members using the material product system of accounts. The committee has acknowledged that in spite of its efforts, factors remain that prevent exact comparability of national accounting aggregates and that most important among the known sources of distortion are "the varied structure of prices within a state and the problems associated with the conversion of national accounts data to a common currency." The committee has tried to take into account real income and has been forced to examine the relevance of existing exchange rates, especially where multiple rate systems have been maintained.

The Committee on Contributions consistently has allowed for disparities in per capita income. For example, as of 1973 states with per capita income below $1,000 were assigned for purposes of assessment a reduction of as much as 50 percent of their computed national income.

Although the committee has noted the difficulties of incorporating adjustments for balance-of-payments difficulties, account sometimes has been taken of the servicing of external debt. Thus, in deriving the scale proposed for 1974-76 the committee reduced assessments for those members who were obligated to allocate a large part of foreign exchange earnings to service foreign debt.

A per capita ceiling principle was available for implementation in all assessment scales after 1956 but in practice has had little impact. The governments of Canada, Denmark, and Sweden volunteered, for example, to forgo the advantage that the principle would have conferred to their peoples during 1974-76. Only the assessments of Kuwait and the United Arab Emirates have been reduced in the 1974-76 scale on the basis of this principle.

Although the principle of adjustment for special circumstances such as heavy losses as a result of catastrophic natural disasters has not played a major role in determining assessment scales, it is still applied on occasion. On the basis of representations made by Hungary, Romania, and the Philippines regarding events of 1969-71, some downward adjustments were made in their 1974-76 assessments.

The regular budget shows some income from sources other than member contributions, namely, payments for administrative services in support of the Expanded Program of Technical Assistance, the high commissioner for refugees, and the United Nations Joint Staff Pension Fund; rental income, reimbursement for staff and services furnished to specialized agencies and others, income from interest and investments, sale of postage stamps and publications, and so on. The preponderant share, however, comes from members' contributions.

Clearly, in determining cost shares for supporting UN programs the overwhelming emphasis was on capacity to pay as indicated by national income per capita. For many purposes this emphasis has operated satisfactorily, but for a number of very important programs, especially peacekeeping, it has led to severe breakdowns and clear opportunities for improvements.

Notes

1. Yet benefits perceived, own and other, may influence, perhaps decisively, the bargaining positions assumed by national representatives. In fact, numerous examples of international cost sharing based wholly or in part on benefits received can be cited. The large share of United Nations Relief and Rehabilitation Administration expenditures borne by the United States apparently reflected desire (or benefit) as well as ability to pay. The quotas for supporting the International Monetary Fund and the World Bank included foreign trade volume. Assessments of members of the European Payments Union were established as simply proportional to the volume of trade with other members of the group. Similarly, the parties to the General Agreement on Tariffs and Trade have assessed each participant according to its share in the total commerce among the signatories.

2. Under certain reasonable conditions, a tendency may be noted toward convergence in the structures of shares appropriate under the apparently diverse principles. That is, if income is positively associated both with individually perceived benefits, a relation described as normal by economists, and with ability to pay, the prescriptions for personal cost shares may be quite similar. Identity of income-benefit and income-ability relations would, of course, be quite fortuitous.

3. One can easily construct a persuasive argument to the effect that ability to pay might take into account availability not only of material income but also of leisure. Consider two individuals who are identical but for a disparity in choices between material income and leisure. Clearly, in an entirely relevant sense the ability to pay of both individuals is the same. Yet if money income is taken as the indicator of ability to pay, the person whose choices lead to more work and therefore to a greater material income will be called upon to contribute more than the one who values leisure more highly. Thus, focusing on ability to pay as measured by money income may discrimate inequitably against certain individuals simply on the basis of their preferences.

4. One way to avoid index number ambiguity while still emphasizing income as a measure of ability to pay would be to specify contributions as percentages of income measured in domestic currencies. The latter approach has serious drawbacks, however, when currencies are not freely convertible.

5. See A. D. Neale. The argument is persuasive when "necessities" are stressed. If discretionary goods are involved it may be reversed (Janet Chapman).

6. See, for example, evidence on perceptions of potential benefits from expanded programs for provision of global goods in Chapter VII, below.

7. Excluding expenditures on peacekeeping, the Korean Reconstruction Agency, Relief for Hungarian Refugees, the specialized trust funds, and the World Bank Group.

8. Resolutions 14 (1) of 13 February 1946, 238 (III) of 18 November 1948, 582 (VI) of 21 December 1951, 665 (VII) of 5 December 1952, 876A (IX) of 4 December 1954; 1137 (XII) of 14 October 1957, 1927 (XVIII) of 11 December 1963, and 2118 (XX) of 21 December 1965, 2654 (XXV) of 4 December 1970, and 2961 B, C, and D (XXVII) of 13 December 1972. See the *Report of the Committee on Contributions* (1973), p. 2.

9. One third of the ordinary expenses (18 November 1948), 30 percent (14 October 1957), 25 percent (13 December 1972).

CHAPTER V

United Nations Financing: Controversy and "Crisis"

A. The Problem

The controversy in the early to mid-1960s over sharing the expenses of the United Nations Emergency Force in the Middle East (UNEF) and the United Nations Operations in the Congo (ONUC) probably was the most spectacular episode in the history of negotiations for global cost sharing. Indeed it was this controversy that brought the organization to a state of financial disarray and semiparalysis that has persisted for well over a decade and promises to persist in one form or another into the foreseeable future. This condition almost guarantees a chronic disability limiting the institution's capacity to administer programs required to carry out even adequately its ostensibly vast responsibilities. The problems almost certainly are not unique, however, but are symptomatic of certain general, delicate issues that modern public microeconomics predicts will arise in connection with sharing.

On first appraisal, the "crisis" over UN financing may seem to be little more than another skirmish in the cold war, a minor battle fought largely by the major contestants as a relatively insignificant episode in their global confrontation. In this view, the primary source of the problem was the conflicting "national interests," and the intensity of the conflict was such that each participant sought avidly to find and to exploit even the most minute of net advantages. Thus, the crisis could be viewed as merely an extension of a pervasive attitude of conflict and confrontation emanating from the general disposition of active adversaries to disagree over virtually every item happening to appear on their agenda.

The general atmosphere of animosity and confrontation doubtlessly did contribute greatly to the problem, but there were other dimensions as well. The question of the role of UN principles and mechanisms seems entirely in order. As we shall see, the clash of "national interests" did not lead inevitably to the financial controversy and crisis. Indeed, upon close examination it seems quite clear that the organization's existing principles and ad hoc mechanisms also were not well suited for coping with the general class of issues to which their application was being attempted.

The emphasis here on problems and on the need for innovative adaptation of mechanisms is by no means intended to denigrate in any way the organization's very considerable accomplishments. True, a succession of conferences, colloquia, behind-the-scenes negotiations, commissions, committees, efforts by the Secretariat, the secretary general, the Security Council, and the General Assembly have made painfully slow progress. Nevertheless, even though advance has been slow and the financial problem in some respects has intensified, it would be unperceptive to insist that absolutely no lessons have been learned and that absolutely no progress has been made. Perhaps the fact deserving the very greatest emphasis is that despite enormous difficulties the mechanisms employed at least allowed the existence of a number of peacekeeping and peacemaking programs very widely regarded as desperately needed.[1] Some demand for them *was* expressed. Contributions *were* sufficient to support activities at meaningful even if in all probability grossly suboptimal[2] levels. The procedures adopted did constitute an enormous stride beyond previous practice. Nevertheless, a rather plausible support can be erected for the proposition that the organization's principles and ad hoc mechanisms interacted almost to guarantee financial malaise.

The UN's experience with international cost sharing seems an especially promising subject for careful economic analysis because of its uniqueness and its great significance. A number of apparently relevant questions come to mind. What was the nature of the United Nations financial problem? What positions were taken by the parties to the controversy? Were the participants in the debate responding in accordance with more general principles of sharing behavior? Why did the procedure that seemed entirely adequate for obtaining revenues for programs financed through the regular budget previously turn out so unsatisfactory for peacekeeping programs? Was it because of a unique attribute of the operations? Or was it due to a characteristic possessed also by other globally collective goods, an attribute that might be expected, therefore, to provoke similar results in superficially different contexts? What features of the UN's financial mechanisms, if any, contributed to the "crisis"? What have been the principal consequences? What lessons have been learned and progress recorded? Have any principles been vindicated (fallen into disrepute)? What is the character of remaining problems? What alterations in the mechanism might be contemplated to respond to these problems? What effects might be anticipated?

1. UNITED NATIONS EMERGENCY FORCE

It will be necessary to review briefly the essential character and circumstances of the United Nations financial problem. Since the creation of UNEF in the mid-1950s and the refusal by a few previously cooperative major economic powers to acknowledge any obligation to respond to United Nations assessments for peacekeeping activities of which they disapproved, the organization has been beset by a financial "problem," in the form of operating deficits, acute illiquidity, and dissipation of its Working Capital Fund. From 1957 through 1962 arrears and defaults amounted to approximately one third of the sums assessed. Governmental voluntary supplements amounted to less than 20 percent of the annual cost of operations, and the deficit in the special account for UNEF was covered by draughts on the Working Capital Fund.

2. UNITED NATIONS CONGO OPERATION

Nevertheless, arrears and defaults on assessments for UNEF could be characterized as "serious" but not a "mortal threat." In conjunction with similar arrears and defaults associated with ONUC, however, the financial situation did become desperate. As of the beginning of the sixteenth session of the General Assembly, forty-one members owed at least a part of their assessments for the 1960 UNEF operations, and sixty-five members owed at least part of their assessments for 1961. The combined deficit for 1960-61 operations was on the order of 25 to 30 percent of the total amount assessed. The ONUC account was even more seriously delinquent. Sixty-six members accounted for a deficit of almost 40 percent of the 1960 assessments. Only twenty-four had paid their 1961 assessments. Two major economic powers, the Soviet Union and France, with assessments on the normal scale amounting to more than 20 percent of the total in 1962, had declared their intention to make no payment, stating rejection of any obligation to submit to the Assembly's request. Most of the defaulting Latin American countries adhered to a less stringent variant of the same position, and many newly admitted members acknowledged a legal obligation but pleaded financial stringency. In the spring of 1963 the Soviet bloc countries announced that they henceforth would withhold a portion of their regular budget assessments attributable to the United Nations Truce Supervision Organization (UNTSO), to the United Nations Commission for the Unification and Rehabilitation of Korea (UNCURK), and to the members of the field service assigned to the Palestine Truce Supervision Organization. Until 1963 funding of such programs had provoked no major protest from the governments of the Soviet bloc countries, although they did object from time to time to paying for UN activities they perceived as inimical to their interests.[3] Thus, it was not until well after the major controversy over the more substantial peacekeeping operations that refusal to respond took place. All told the deficits continued to mount from that time forward. By the beginning of 1974, the organization did not possess sufficient cash resources to pay its current debts to national governments for goods and services previously rendered. If the organization were to attempt to pay these debts, after completely emptying its treasury, after exhausting the Working Capital Fund, the Bond Account, and the Special Account, it still would be short $23.7 million.[4] During 1973 current obligations (including payrolls) were being met by borrowing from other accounts, such as the Tax Equalization Fund, the construction accounts, and the Special Account *(Financial Report 1973,* p. 2).

This account was established in September 1965 to receive from member states contributions intended to alleviate or, hopefully, to eliminate the organization's financial difficulties. Through January 10, 1974, twenty-four member states contributed over $37 million *(Financial Report 1973,* p. 15). The government of Japan, contributor of $10 million, expressed the hope that other states might be induced thereby to make contributions of magnitude sufficient to achieve a definitive solution to the organization's financial problem *(Financial Report 1973,* p. 34).

Another view of the organization's financial status as of December 31, 1973, is available in Table 2, which shows the short-term deficit amounted to either $70.8 million or $87.5 million, depending on the scope of the concept employed. Further small additions to the deficit associated with UNEF 1973 for about two months of 1973 were anticipated *(Financial Report 1973,* p. 7). And, in fact, these anticipations were quickly realized. Unpaid contributions for the first eighteen months of UNEF 1973 amounted to $49 million. Of this almost $8 million was due from four member states that had let it be known that they felt no obligation to contribute *(United Nations Monthly Chronicle,* May 1975, p. 5).

By the beginning of 1974, consistent with their opposition to supporting certain items in the regular budget sixteen members states had withheld an estimated $41 million.[5] Assessed constrifutions toward the

TABLE 2
SHORT-TERM DEFICIT OF THE UNITED NATIONS AS OF
DECEMBER 31, 1973[a]
(MILLIONS OF U.S. DOLLARS)

Regular Budget and Working Capital Fund	
Amounts withheld on principle	57.9[b]
United Nations Emergency Force	
Conditional contributions repayable to governments	0.6
Obligations in excess of assessed contributions, voluntary contributions, and miscellaneous income available	38.9
Less financed from:	
Bonds	(8.1)
Special Account[c]	(3.9)
Net Obligations	27.5
United Nations Operation in the Congo	
Conditional contributions repayable to governments	1.6
Obligations in excess of assessed contributions, voluntary contributions, and miscellaneous income available	48.4
Less: Financed from bonds	(35.9)
Net Obligations	14.1
Total Gross Deficit	99.5
Less contributions and pledges to Special Account	28.7[d]
Net Deficit ("A" Concept)	70.8
Add: Amounts due Member States from surplus accounts[e] for contributions to:	
UNEF	1.1
ONUC	15.6
	16.7
Net Deficit ("B" Concept)	87.5

[a] Adapted from United Nations, General Assembly, *Official Records: Report of the Special Committee on the Financial Situation of the United Nations*, twenty-seventh session, Suppl. 29 (A/8729), 1972 and from *Financial Report 1973*, p. 8.

[b] Includes $16.6 million from the government of China prior to October 25, 1971.

[c] General Assembly resolution 2115 (XX).

[d] Excludes $10 million receivable for the purposes of resolution 3049A (XXVII), contributed conditional on response of other member states.

[e] See *Report of the Ad Hoc Committee of Experts to Examine the Finances of the United Nations and the Specialized Agencies* (A/6289), March 28, 1966, pp. 12 ff., for detailed defenses of the alternative concepts.

regular budget outstanding on December 31, 1973, included an additional $14.3 million owed by governments not withholding on the basis of principle *(Financial Report 1973,* p. 141).

Further unpaid assessed contributions are outstanding in connection with the Special Account for the United Nations Emergency Force and the Ad Hoc Account for the United Nations Operation in the Congo. As of the beginning of 1974, they amounted, respectively, to $44 million and $75 million. The preponderant shares of these amounts had been assessed thirteen members that indicated quite explicitly their unwillingness to respond. In addition, without stating unwillingness in principle, nine members simply made no payments on $1.7 million in assessments for UNEF, and nineteen members simply made no payments on $4.2 million in assessments for ONUC *(Financial Report 1973,* p. 142). [6]

B. Report of the Special Committee on the Financial Situation of the United Nations

The status of thought of the Secretariat and the representatives of member states on the financial problem of the organization as of the early 1970s is well summarized in the *Report of the Special Committee on the Financial Situation of the United Nations.*[7] In December 1971 the General Assembly charged the Special Committee with submitting suggestions and concrete proposals for resolving the organization's financial problem.

The committee analyzed the problem into three interrelated components: illiquidity, indefinitely prolonged withholding of assessed contributions, and the accumulated debt. In the committee's view the organization's illiquidity required immediate measures. This problem was in fact alleviated when a substantial number of member governments responded to appeals from the secretary general and from the Special Committee to pay their assessed contributions to the regular budget earlier than previously.

Regarding creation of a mechanism for elimination of withholding, the report states that an understanding was reached among twelve of the fifteen members of the Special Committee on a set of proposals and that almost all members preferred the existing method of financing the items contained in the regular budget but were willing to make concessions if they would facilitate resolution of the problem.

The essence of the proposals included the following:

(1) Three contested items—the United Nations Memorial Cemetery in Korea, the United Nations Commission for the Unification

and Rehabilitation of Korea, and the repayment of the United Nations bond issue—would be deleted from the expenditure sections of the regular budget. They would be financed instead from miscellaneous income.

(2) Technical aid programs might be removed from the regular budget on the understanding that they would be financed, undiminished, from contributions to the United Nations Development Programme.[8]

(3) All members from 1973 would agree to pay in full all assessments for the regular budget.

(4) The accumulated short-term deficit would be settled once and for all.

Representatives of the USSR and Poland expressed dissenting views. They declared their opposition to using budgetary income under the heading, "Miscellaneous Income," to cover expenditures for interest and amortization of UN bonds, UNCURK, or the Memorial Cemetery in Korea. The Soviet representative indicated further that the Western powers and their allies should relinquish their claims for repayment of the bonds, and redemption of those held by developing countries should be accomplished from voluntary contributions. He did concur in the proposal that technical assistance items be removed from the regular budget and added that the currencies in which contributions to the United Nations Development Programme were made should be at the discretion of the contributor.

C. The Situation as of December 1973

Regarding elimination of the accumulated deficit, there was general agreement in the Special Committee that the major part of the deficit could be eliminated only by voluntary contributions from member states, including through creditors' relinquishing of claims. A number of representatives stressed the collective responsibility of all members. One representative pointed out that an agreement among the permanent members of the Security Council was necessary. Thus, the clash between adherents to the doctrine of collective responsibility and those of individual state sovereignty continued to frustrate efforts to resolve the financial problem of the Organization. The situation as seen by the Secretariat as of December 1973 was summarized as follows: "the key ingredient necessary for the solution of . . . the Organization's financial problems has not yet been found, namely, the way to eliminate completely the withholding of contributions assessed upon member states by the General Assembly," *(Report of the Secretary-General on the Financial Situation of the United Nations,* December 11, 1973, A/9444, p. 4).

1. ADEQUACY OF AD HOC MEASURES

In spite of the unresolved financial problem, ad hoc measures proved adequate to support certain peacekeeping operations even after the acrimonious debates and financial crisis of the early 1960s. Most notably, beginning in 1964 financial support for the United Nations Force in Cyprus (UNFICYP) was obtained from unassessed contributions but "with great difficulty" (Russell, p. 346). The Security Council approved an expanded observer group in Kashmir in 1965, thereby permitting financing through the regular budget. The problem of financing UNEF for 1965 and 1966 was approached as follows. The arrangement was explicitly labeled ad hoc to avoid any clash with any member's position of principle. Expenditures were apportioned *(not assessed)* on a special scale, with all but 2.4 percent to be paid by the twenty-six nations classified as developed in 1963. Less developed countries were to contribute the remainder. Within the two groups member shares were calculated according to the proportions established for the regular budget. In anticipation of continued refusals to pay by certain governments a "reserve" was established. In December 1966 a similar ad hoc solution was adopted to support UNEF in 1967 and again when it was reconstituted as UNEF II in 1973. The two major operations since the financial crisis of the early 1960s, UNFICYP and UNEF II, merit examination in a bit more detail.

2. UN FORCE IN CYPRUS

On March 4, 1964, even before the last ONUC contingent had departed the Congo, the Security Council authorized another peacekeeping operation, the United Nations Force in Cyprus. The authorizing resolution recommended that all costs pertaining to the force be met "in a manner to be agreed upon . . . by the Governments providing the contingents and by the Government of Cyprus. The Secretary-General may also accept voluntary contributions for that purpose." [9]

The wording of the resolution shows recognition that under some circumstances "collective responsibility" was not an applicable principle. The operation would have to be supported by those who perceived sufficient potential benefit to make the sacrifice worthwhile. There would be no point in assessing the rest and spending goodwill, trust, and diplomatic resources in further confrontation over financial support.

The formula, although not completely satisfactory as we shall see presently, did permit support of UNFICYP from 1964 to the present.[10] According to estimates by Wainhouse, through 1969 the nine countries providing contingents [11] absorbed $62 million of $149 million total costs for UNFICYP (p. 411). The remainder was, of course, to be covered by financial contributions. Countries with special interest in resolving the conflict were major contributors. Specifically, together the United States and the United Kingdom provided approximately two thirds of the total financial contribution.[12] Less affluent countries with special interests in the area, Greece and Turkey, also were significant financial contributors.

But in spite of these positive accomplishments, considerable room for improvement remains. In the annual financial reports of the organization, the Board of Auditors repeatedly has called attention to "unsatisfactory financial arrangements." For example, in the report for the period ending on December 31, 1973, they stated:

> Ever since the United Nations commenced its peace-keeping role in Cyprus . . . , the financial arrangements have proved to be unsatisfactory, because the Secretary-General has no authority to use funds other than voluntary contributions, which have been insufficient to meet the costs of the Force. Over the period from 27 March 1964 to 31 December 1973, these costs have totalled $167.3 million, exclusive of extra costs absorbed by Governments providing contingents which are estimated to have exceeded $50.8 million through 31 December 1973. The Secretary-General received voluntary contributions from 51 member states and four non-member governments during the nine-year period which, together with miscellaneous income, totalled $139.9 million. This shortfall in cash resources of $27.4 million at 31 December 1973 remains to be financed from future voluntary contributions. Unpaid pledges recorded in the accounts at 31 December 1973 of $6.7 million are expected to be realized in due course.
>
> During 1973, only 23 Governments paid a total of $13,267,302 against pledges made in 1973 and prior years. Obligations incurred during the year approximated $15,450,000, of which only $4,784,423 was recorded in the accounts. This increased to $22,065,000 the obligations which have not been included in the accounts because of lack of funds. (United Nations, General Assembly, *Official Records: Financial Report and Accounts for the Year Ended 31 December 1973* and *Report of the Board of Auditors*, Twenty-ninth Session, Suppl. 7. [A/9607].)

The secretaries general likewise have reiterated misgivings, if not downright dismay, over the arrangements for financing UNFICYP. Indeed, by June 1964, even before the problem actually materialized, the secretary general had declared, "the method of financing the Force in Cyprus . . . is most unsatisfactory. . . . There is a large degree of uncertainty about what will be actually available, and therefore planning . . . [is] sorely hampered" (UN Doc. S/5764, June 15, 1964, par. 127; cited in Stegenga, p. 169). And a few months later he "complained that the method had worked so poorly 'as to make planning, efficiency and economical running of the Force almost impossible' " (Stegenga, p. 169). The mechanism indeed placed an onerous burden on the secretary general, who was obliged to accept responsibility for explaining and searching for a way out of a financial dilemma created by the member governments, which themselves were either unwilling or unable to resolve the problem (Stegenga, pp. 170 ff.). Appeals for more money and declarations of intent to recommend reductions in the force have emanated regularly from the secretary general's office through the life of UNFICYP. For example, after approximately a decade of experience the secretary general still was pointing out the seriousness of the deficit, the main reason for which he claimed was "the insufficiency of voluntary contributions which had continued to come from a disappointingly limited number of Governments" *(United Nations Monthly Chronicle,* January 1975, p. 4).

In sum, the UNFICYP has been supported by voluntary contributions, financial and in kind, and by involuntary contributions by the organization's creditors, so to say, resulting from its inability to fulfill obligations to reimburse according to agreement. Thus, the obligations of the organization again have grown more rapidly than the wherewithal to meet them, a relation that is understandably distressing to the Secretariat, especially considered in the context of the organization's overall financial status. While the contributions enumerated above, and especially the maintenance of UNFICYP for more than a decade, easily can be regarded as an impressive achievement, remaining defects in the financial mechanisms are very readily apparent.

3. UNEF II, UN DISENGAGEMENT OBSERVER FORCE

On October 25, 1973, the Security Council established UNEF II. Cost-sharing arrangements for the force were spelled out in the General Assembly's resolution 3101 (XXVIII), which appropriated $30 million for the period October 25, 1973-April 24, 1974. Essentially, the costs were to be shared by economically developed states, with token contributions by the others. The five permanent members of the Security Council were to be responsible for almost two thirds of the total, leaving approximately one third for the rest of the economically developed member states. Within groups, states were called upon to pay in the same proportion as for the regular budget. Voluntary contributions also were invited. Resolution 3101 was adopted by a vote of 108 to 3, with 1 abstention, and only the representatives of Albania, Lybia, and Syria voting against it, suggesting a consensus that augured well for avoiding a large disparity between expenditures on and revenues for UNEF II. Of the permanent members of the Security Council, only China indicated unwillingness to accept the indicated share. This same pattern of cost sharing has been followed to meet expenses under subsequent appropriations for UNEF 1973 and for the United Nations Disengagement Observer Force (UNDOF) *(United Nations Monthly Chronicle,* December 1974, pp. 66 ff.).

Past experience suggests, nevertheless, that the UNEF II and UNDOF accounts will show some deficit. If they do, it will not be the first time that voting on resolutions will appear inconsistent with subsequent fiscal response or that voluntary contributions fail to offset the refusal of a permanent member of the Security Council to respond to an "assessment."

Thus, it appears that the modes for financing UNEF II, UNDOF, and UNFICYP reflected accommodations to fit circumstances peculiar to each. The assessment scale that in all probability will work reasonably well for UNEF II and UNDOF almost certainly would have been acceptable neither to the Soviet bloc countries nor to China for UNFICYP. The voluntary system that permitted the existence of UNFICYP for over a decade probably would not have permitted indication of so firm a commitment to UNEF II and UNDOF as the system actually employed.

The simultaneous authorization of appropriations and declarations of agreement on cost shares for UNEF II was an important step forward in the rationality of decision making. Rationality could be advanced still further by simultaneous establishment of early deadlines for actual transfer of funds, so that expenditures on programs could be restricted to payments actually received. Furthermore, a modest contingency fund would seem only prudent.

Notably absent in the formula for sharing the costs of UNEF II is recognition of special benefit to the parties most directly involved. As may be verified with the aid of data in Table 3, the principal adversaries were called upon to pay less than 0.2 percent of the total assessments, that is, amounts even more minuscule compared with their national military expenditures.

D. Resistance of Recalcitrant Powers

From the early 1960s to the present the recalcitrant powers withstood various attempts to induce their acceptance of an obligation to abide by General Assembly votes authorizing assessments to share the costs of

TABLE 3. ASSESSMENTS FOR UNEF 1973[a]

Country	(Dollars)	Percent of National Defense Expenditure for 1973[b]	Defense Expenditures[b] (dollars)
Algeria	4,810	.0010	404,000,000
Egypt	7,214	.0004	1,737,000,000
Iran	12,025	.0006	2,010,000,000
Iraq	3,006	—	—
Israel	12,626	.0008	1,474,000,000
Jordan	1,202	—	—
Lebanon	1,804	—	—
Libyan Arab Republic	6,613	.0046	145,000,000
Morocco	3,607	—	—
Saudi Arabia	3,607	.0003	1,090,000,000
Sudan	600	—	—
Syrian Arab Republic	1,202	.0006	216,000,000
Tunisia	1,202	—	—

[a] United Nations, General Assembly, *Official Records: Financial Report and Accounts for the Year Ended 31 December 1973,* twenty-ninth session, Suppl. 7 (A/9607), pp. 85-87.

[b] The Military Balance 1973-74, 1974-75.

peacekeeping programs. Specifically there were attempts: to apply the Article 19 sanction,[13] to cajole through a World Court advisory opinion to the effect that the assessments were legally binding, to apply unremitting diplomatic pressure through appeals to the principle of collective responsibility, and to secure support through the bond issue.

1. THE BOND ISSUE

Consider first their refusal to subscribe to the UN bond issue. In December 1961 the General Assembly by a vote of 58 to 13 (24 abstentions, 9 absent) authorized the secretary general to issue $200 million worth of bonds in order to cover outstanding obligations connected with disputed expenditures.[14] This resort to deferred payment ostensibly was an emergency measure intended primarily to alleviate the financial distress and to reduce the antagonisms of a severely divided membership. But both principal and interest were to be repaid as an item in the regular budget and therefore were to be apportioned according to the regular scale. As Stoessinger et al. point out, these measures were "not only to ensure collective responsibility but also to make certain that Article 19 could be invoked against defaulting member states" (p. 125).

Other potential effects of the bond issue were perceived by various parties. Since bonds might be offered to members of the specialized agencies and to other institutions, an additional source of revenue might be developed. But, on the other hand, some thought that bond purchasers in effect would reduce the pressure on states in arrears, thereby promoting continued "fiscal irresponsibility." The bond issue might in fact very substantially postpone the time at which Article 19 could be invoked. Perhaps not very surprisingly the recalcitrant powers perceived the bond issue as a not very devious ruse to inveigle their support for the programs they already had rejected so emphatically. And they responded in at least a comparatively forthright fashion by refusing to buy any bonds and later by deducting from their contributions to the regular budget amounts attributable to the bond issue.[15]

Thus, the bond issue did little to resolve the basic problem and did prolong the agonizing over the organization's financial deficit.

2. RESPONSE TO THE WORLD COURT ADVISORY OPINION

The response of the recalcitrant powers to the World Court advisory opinion fit very closely their overall pattern of resistance. Their adversaries, the staunch adherents of the principle of collective responsibility, argued that the disputed operations had been legally constituted in accordance with the appropriate division of duties and responsibilities of the General Assembly and the Security Council and that Article 17 specified that the Assembly had authority to make assessments for "legitimate expenses of the organization."

Critics, especially the representatives of the Soviet government, argued that assessments for both UNEF and ONUC were illegal because only the Security Council legitimately could have authorized such operations and their financing. They held that Article 17 pertained only to the administrative budget and not to the special peacekeeping accounts. The Soviet government suggested an alternative method of finance, namely, the "aggressors" should pay all of the costs. Many Latin American governments took the less abrasive stand that peacekeeping expenses should not be regarded as normal expenses and that therefore a special assessment scale would be appropriate.

In December 1961 the General Assembly requested an advisory opinion from the International Court of Justice (ICJ) in the hope it would facilitate a resolution of the conflict. In July 1962 the ICJ declared its belief that the disputed expenditures "constituted 'expenses of the Organization' within the meaning of Article 17, paragraph 2 of the Charter." [16] The General Assembly formally "accepted" the opinion by a vote of 76 to 17 (8 abstentions).

Some governments responded to the opinion and paid previously contested assessments, but the major recalcitrants explicitly rejected it and continued their refusal to accept the levies.

3. THE ARTICLE 19 CONTROVERSY

They also weathered an attempt to apply the Article 19 sanction for the nineteenth session of the Assembly,[17] although their accumulated arrears apparently made its application appropriate. By December 1964 the arrears of twelve members, including the Soviet Union and France, were large enough to raise the possibility of applying the sanction, and the U.S. government endeavored to accomplish just that. Although the support for "collective responsibility" was quite extensive, it was not sufficiently intensive to support application of the sanction in the face of adamant opposition. The U.S. executive branch, while maintaining the legality of its position, agreed in mid-1965 to withdraw its pressure for application of Article 19 in the subsequent General Assembly. Since then, although arrears have mounted further, the applicability of the Article 19 sanction has not been raised again.

4. THE RESCUE FUND

Although on occasion some of the reluctant powers hinted, and even declared that under certain conditions they might be willing to make contributions to the Rescue Fund, somehow the conditions never were met, and no contributions were forthcoming. What was the Rescue Fund? It was one result of an ad hoc arrangement designed to attain a compromise on a cost-sharing formula for UNEF and ONUC for the latter part of 1963 (Russell, p. 336). The arrangement was as follows. A portion, $5.5 million, of the estimated costs were to be apportioned according to the regular scale for all members. The remaining expenses, $37 million, were to be largely the obligation of the developed countries, since they were called upon: (1) to comply again with a regular assessment; and (2) to make up through "voluntary contributions" for a 55 percent reduction in the assessments of the "economically less developed countries" (A/Res. 1875 [S-IV] and A/Res. 1876 [S-IV] 6-27-63; cited in Russell, p. 336). This compromise was not agreed to by the French and Soviet governments, which refused to contribute and indeed continued to make contributions to the regular budget as they saw fit, rather than according to assessments.

For 1964 the General Assembly voted further sizable expenditures for UNEF. Costs were to be shared according to an ad hoc formula similar to that for the latter part of 1963.[18] Major potential contributors were not satisfied with these compromises, and it was only to be expected that difficulties would arise in the attempts to implement them. The United

States in particular declared that its voluntary contributions would depend upon similar donations from other members [19] (U.S. Department of State, *Bulletin,* vol. 54 [1966], p. 210; cited in Russell, p. 346). Whereas in 1965 the secretary general had announced that approximately $100 million would be required to meet existing obligations and to replenish the Working Capital Fund, only $23 million had been given by February 1967 (Russell, p. 388).[20]

E. Principle, Tactics and Ideological Incongruities

Although the controversy over financing UN peacekeeping operations may be regarded as a unique historical episode to be understood in its entirety only in terms of special circumstances, personalities, initiatives, responses, and interactions, it is tempting to look for potentially useful general guidelines for sharing that may have been enunciated by the participants. Of course the adversaries did cite "principles" to bolster their legal and bureaucratic positions. Their arguments constituted, however, no disinterested analyses relevant to attainment of globally efficient and equitable states of the world. They constituted basically tactical measures to promote the net advantage of the adversaries themselves.

1. U.S. SUPPORT FOR "COLLECTIVE RESPONSIBILITY."

This dominance of tactics resulted in some striking incongruities with very well established ideological positions. The American government, noted for its devotion to rugged individualism, under the circumstances found high virtue in "collective responsibility," a slogan frequently referred to, but rarely spelled out, but in effect a brand of international collectivism bound to be viewed as unacceptably tyrannical by the minority. It seems to mean that all members must abide by decisions reached according to constitutional voting rules and must make whatever material sacrifice is called for, no matter how inefficient, inequitable, or onerous dissenters may perceive it to be. The values held by dissenting members of the organization were to be subordinated to the "will" of the rest as revealed by the votes cast in favor of or against the program in question and the cost shares needed for its implementation.

2. USES FOR COLLECTIVE RESPONSIBILITY.

Several uses of the doctrine might be perceived. Appeal to collective responsibility may be viewed as a form of "moral suasion" to aid in securing an efficient and equitable distribution of benefit and cost shares. In this view, the outputs of the program are international peace and security that provide a benefit to all and to which, therefore, all must contribute. The appeal to collective responsibility is simply an appeal for everyone to do his "fair share," to defend against the would-be free rider.

The stress on collective responsibility may be viewed somewhat differently, namely, its proponents may reason that a contract is a contract and that signing the Charter in fact amounted to acceptance of the distribution of sacrifices specified by the Assembly, no matter what the perception of distribution of benefits. Thus, although the lines of thought are different, the conclusions are the same. Collective responsibility requires acceptance of the sacrifice voted by the General Assembly.

3. SOVIET INDIVIDUALISM

For its part, the Soviet government, normally an avid supporter of thoroughgoing collectivism, found necessary a staunch defense of its individual rights, that is, the right to reject a collective decision, in the face of the onslaught of a distasteful brand of collective tyranny rather passionately championed by the normally more individualistically inclined Americans.[21] Soviet official concern was prompted, of course, by the fact that it was *their* rights, *their* decision-making prerogative that was being infringed upon. Needless to say, their individualism did not extend to allowing Soviet citizens to decide for themselves how much they thought UN programs were worth and to decide on their own contributions.

In essence, the issue was who was to have the last word with regard to the appropriate size for a member's contribution, the individual state's government exercising its sovereignty, or the collectivity voting under procedures established by the Charter. Thus, collective responsibility constituted an emphatic challenge to the independence of the individual states.

4. WESTERN RESERVATIONS ABOUT COLLECTIVE RESPONSIBILITY

The major deviation, the apparently steadfast devotion of the American executive branch to collective responsibility, seemed especially curious. Clearly, in other easily imaginable circumstances American enthusiasm for the principle would be far less pronounced.[22] No government, the United States no more than others, can be expected to sacrifice heavily in support of programs perceived as strongly inimical to its people's "interest." Under such conditions U.S. government officials undoubtedly would hasten to abandon this particular form of international collectivism and assert a doctrine of individual state sovereignty more in keeping with their traditional emphasis on individual rights in domestic affairs. Strict adherence to collective responsibility would imply, for example, that the General Assembly could levy assessments for transfers of income and wealth that might be anathema to citizens of the developed countries (Russell, p. 343). Assessments might be made for economic development projects in adversary countries or in countries maintaining cordial relations with them. Thus, if American officials had succeeded in obtaining complete acceptance of collective responsibility, any denial of obligation to support other international organizational programs would have become even more awkward, to say the least.

The potential disadvantages of too strict application of this doctrine have been acknowledged in published form by various Western spokesmen. As early as 1952 the U.S. Congress had indicated explicitly that it, not the General Assembly, would have the last word in specifying the size of U.S. contributions to the UN (Russell, p. 340). Western authors, Daniel S. Cheever and H. Field Haviland (cited in Stoessinger et al., pp. 151-52), recognized quite clearly the limitations of collective responsibility, no matter what its legal foundations, and the importance rather of the distribution and intensity of perceived benefits. They wrote in reference to General Assembly resolutions: "It is not so much their legal character as 'recommendations' which determines their effectiveness but rather the quality, quantity, and intensity of community support behind them." Justice Fitzmaurice stated in support of the World Court advisory opinion that: (1) "although given expenditures [were] expenses of the Organization, there may not necessarily or always be an obligation for every Member State to contribute to them"; (2) "expenses of the United Nations" could broadly be divided into obligatory and permissive categories, peacekeeping belonging to the former and economic and social measures to the latter; and (3) "The Assembly could vote enormous expenditures, and thereby place a heavy financial burden even on dissenting states, and as a matter of obligation even in the case of nonessential activities." [23] Thus, Justice Fitzmaurice judged applicability of collective responsibility on the basis of the essentiality of the programs to which it might be applied. But essence, like benefits and beauty, notoriously is in the eye of the beholder. Sovereign decision makers will not support programs in which they perceive harm, or at least little benefit, no matter how essential they may appear to others.

The Fitzmaurice doctrine was exceedingly convenient for the Western governments, since it called for adherence to collective responsibility in the peacekeeping operations that they were likely to support, while at the same time allowing an escape from a similar obligation for any economic and social programs not to their liking. Of course, the West could not have it both ways and indeed was as unable to obtain adherence to collective responsibility in support of the peacekeeping programs as it would have been unwilling to accept collective responsibility for any program in which it perceived no benefit. But Justice Fitzmaurice, to his credit, did recognize, and call attention to, the injustice and unwork-ability of placing a heavy financial burden on dissenting states, the principle of collective responsibility to the contrary notwithstanding.

U.S. officials have publicly recognized the weaknesses and the potential for certain undesirable applications of collective responsibility to the United States. They also have recognized some advantage in permitting opting out for others. U.S. Ambassador to the United Nations Goldberg stated in the General Assembly's Special Political Committee on November 24, 1965, the American preference for "full collective responsibility [as] the first choice," but he also declared that "an opting-out arrangement for permanent members as an interim measure" [24] was acceptable.

Representatives O'Hara and Frelinghuysen argued that: "the United States should be prepared to contribute financially whatever is required to support United Nations peacekeeping operations of which it approves"; "it follows . . . that the United States should be able to 'opt out' of operations to which we object." [25] According to Assistant Secretary of State Sisco, "Those of us who think that a peacekeeping operation is . . . desirable . . . and want to support it financially will have to do it . . . either by a pure and simple voluntary contribution . . . or by apportioning the cost among . . . the countries who support that particular peacekeeping operation." [26] And in practice the insistence on collective responsibility was abandoned to avoid further unproductive haggling on at least one occasion, namely, in settling arrangements for UNFICYP.

Thus, experience has demonstrated the limited utility of dogged adherence to "collective responsibility," and to their credit its early adherents have recognized that, at least in certain circumstances, its disadvantages may outweigh its advantages.[27]

Collective responsibility may have some usefulness as a bargaining slogan. Its efficacy in all probability will be strictly limited, however, because of its violation of a compellingly convincing corollary to the more general principle of human propensities to make decisions in self-interest. It can be stated with great confidence that human beings making decisions in their own self-interest or on behalf of their constituents will not willingly sacrifice goods for something they regard as a bad. Similarly, members of a sharing group will resist impositions of incremental cost shares in excess of marginal benefits received. They will search for means to avoid sacrifices requested of them by other members of the group.

There may be circumstances under which a sharer will not even accept incremental cost shares that equal the marginal benefits received. Especially where adversaries are concerned, a sharing scheme may be refused because, even though both groups gain, one (or both, for that matter) may suspect that his adversary is gaining relatively. Whether there is a clearly objective relative gain, or a subjective asymmetry in perception of the distribution of net benefits, difficulties may arise in connection with sharing by adversaries. Thus, one or more parties may be expected to resist a sharing scheme, search for an alternative, or even to break a contract, particularly so general an obligation as Article 17 of the Charter.

Of course, it is not only when adversaries are sharing that such difficulties may arise. Congenial sharers also may be concerned with equity. If a proposed distribution of cost shares, based, let's say, merely on capacity to pay, creates a distribution of *net* benefits that some members perceive as inequitable, a problem may well arise in securing the cooperation necessary for implementation. The well-known subjectivity in perception of equity is of course no help, even among friends, in facilitating an agreement.

It is probably true that many decision makers will accept comparatively small assessments for support of a "bad" in the interest of harmony, goodwill, and a spirit of compromise. Sheer inertia also may become involved, that is, effort to come to a decision and to defend a position may be large enough to make worthwhile toleration of the nuisance to avoid the effort necessary to eliminate it. But assessments beyond a certain threshhold in all probability will encounter resistance from the reluctant party, and the extensiveness and intensiveness of efforts at avoidance will depend upon the magnitudes of the sacrifices requested and the degree of perceived unpalatability of the program.[28] This is in principle a testable behavioral proposition. Actual tests clearly are remote, however, not least because of the difficulty in obtaining data on perceived marginal benefits.

5. SOVIET ADVOCACY OF FLEXIBLE RESPONSE

The views of the principal opponent of collective responsibility are, of course, of special interest. Throughout the numerous discussions in the UN the Soviet government objected to what it claimed were rigid mechanisms for supporting peacekeeping (Weiner, p. 927). Its representatives mentioned billing the aggressors, sharing costs among the entire UN membership, sharing by parties to the conflict, voluntary contributions, or a combination of the above, as possible alternatives depending on the circumstances. Of course, such ad hoc approaches incorporate no well-articulated rationale, no clear statement of goals, and no well-conceived theoretical framework linking goals and instruments thought capable of facilitating their attainment. Soviet advocacy of flexibility, no less than

American devotion to collective responsibility, clearly constituted a mere tactic to advance their more general short-term purposes.[29] Undoubtedly if the circumstances in which the governmental representatives found themselves had been reversed, they would have exchanged tactics, too. Any sovereign decision maker will reject requests for sacrifices in support of undesired programs, especially if in the process he is able to impede the program itself. And this may be the vital principle relevant to sharing costs of international security programs.

In sum, UN fiscal mechanisms for peacekeeping operations have included attempts at application of the assessment scale established for the regular budget and later of ad hoc compromise scales that also proved to command less than universal assent.[30] Also included were frankly voluntary contributions. Finally, involuntary [31] contributions accounted for a significant portion of the total support.

The following list indicates the means of financing various UN peacekeeping operations through December 1971:

Regular Budget Assessments
  UNTSO (May 1948-December 1971)
  The United Nations Military Observer Groups in India and Pakistan (January 1949-December 1971)
  The United Nations Observer Group in Lebanon (June 1958-December 1958)
  The United Nations India-Pakistan Observation Mission (September 1965-March 1966)
Special Account, Voluntary Contributions, Involuntary Contributions,[32] Bonds
  UNEF (November 1956-May 1967)
  ONUC (July 1060-July 1964)
Voluntary Contributions
  UNFICYP (March 1964-December 1971)
By Parties to Agreement
  The United Nations in West New Guinea (September 1962-May 1963)
  The United Nations Yemen Observation Mission (June 1963-September 1964)

The minuteness of the distinction between voluntary contributions and assessments may not be readily apparent, but it is indeed minute, since the latter in fact have been paid essentially on the volition of the members. The difference appears to be in the formal locus of final authority in specifying an amount and, from a legal point of view, the applicability of sanctions. Assessments involve a presumption that the final authority lies with the members of the organization and that the decision reached by voting in the Assembly will be binding on each national government, with recalcitrants subject to penalties that make compliance more attractive. Where the penalites are small relative to the sacrifice requested, and where the potential costs to the membership of attempts at applying the sanctions are great, the actual contribution obtained from any given member is likely to approximate closely the amount that could be negotiated under a purely voluntary cost-sharing mechanism.

F. UN Financial Problem and Public Mircoeconomics

How can the UN's financial problems be understood from the viewpoint of public microeconomic theory? The peacekeeping programs undoubtedly did possess, in significant degree, public good properties. To provide funds for them, the majority espoused an essentially organic interpretation of the public good and the doctrine of collective responsibility. In harmony with this approach, capacity to pay became the appropriate criterion for determining assessment. The primary difficulty— rejection of assessments by major potential contributors—might be regarded as just another manifestation of free-riding. But the rejections also can be regarded as attempts to avoid forced rides.

The crucial issue is the benefits (?) perceived by recalcitrant parties relative to their assessments. If they in fact were striving to ride free, insistence on collective responsibility was consistent with an attempt to attain a workable approximation to an efficient and presumably equitable set of cost shares. If, on the other hand, their intent was to avoid forced rides, insistence on collective responsibility would seem to have served little useful purpose. From the perspective of the modern theory of sharing, the UN's experience of recent years strongly suggests that more careful attention to the distribution of benefits will facilitate better understanding and more effective global sharing.

It was asserted above that the organization's financial procedures interacted almost to guarantee malaise. What, more precisely, constitutes the case for that proposition?

The vagueness of the Charter permitted its apparent consistency with the incompatible doctrines of collective responsibility and national sovereignty. Thus, one might be tempted to conclude that the vagueness was at the root of the clash between supporters of the two incompatible principles. In fact, it may have contributed to the confusion and controversy but probably was not decisive. Leaders of powerful sovereign states doubtlessly would find bases for resisting calls for collective responsibility even if the concept had been stated in detail, precisely and explicitly in the Charter.

It seems rather that two interdependent factors interact to create the organization's deficits. They are: (1) adamant adherence to collective responsibility for a distribution of assessments based largely on capacity to pay and strongly violating some members' perceptions of equity in the distribution of net benefits; and (2) absence of simultaneity in decisions about program levels and the distribution of cost sharing with specified dating of contributions. By itself, violation of perceived equity would not lead to severe difficulties if the level of programs were considered simultaneously with cost shares and curtailed to reflect refusals to accept them. Similarly, by itself lack of simultaneity in decision making would not create a crisis [33] if the distribution of assessments were recognized universally as "reasonably" equitable and efficient. The presence of both, however, spells trouble for the organization, since it results in the capability for authorizing programs for which agreement on cost shares subsequently cannot be attained.[34] Thus, the UN's financial difficulties may stem more from too strong support for faulty principles than, as sometimes has been maintained, from too weak support for a sound one. The inadequacies of these principles were almost bound to appear as soon as they were applied to facilitate sharing the sacrifices for programs of any sort—peacekeeping, development, or whatever beyond the most nominal.

G. Role of Mechanisms

Attainment of a mechanism that can be relied upon to account for the distribution of net benefits admittedly is in only the very beginning of its development. Efficiency and equity in global cost and benefit sharing will require further development of such mechanisms, and ultimately they may contribute to rationality of such sharing. For the immediate future, however, other expedients can be relied upon. Namely, for the time being activities can be constrained for consistency with revenues implied by cost shares and payment time schedules agreed upon simultaneously with authorization of expenditures. The programs agreed upon may or may not [35] be less ambitious. But a point of contention will have been avoided, as will the image of impotence, disarray, and confusion.

An indirect consquence of the organization's mechanisms remains to be noted. The upshot of the financial controversy and crisis has been that minority opponents of UN programs have been able by indirect means to have their cake and eat it too. Not only have they avoided contributions themselves, but through the financial controversy and crisis they were able to impede, or even in effect veto, implementation of programs that had been voted in spite of their opposition (Russell, p. 333). As Ruth Russell has very perceptively noted,

> Although failing in this direct attack, the Soviet Union succeeded by indirect means in eventually achieving much of its objective of curtailing the activities of the Assembly and the Secretary-General in the peace and security field . . . when the U.S. allowed peacekeeping activities to become dependent on financial support from opponents of those operations, which was what happened as the Article 19 crisis evolved. The U.S. had the weakest possible negotiating position, since the Soviet Union and France literally needed to do *nothing* to obtain what they wanted. (p. 333)

Thus, the regular budgetary mechanism for determining the level for UN programs and for allocating cost shares produced clearly negative effects when attempts were made to apply it to meet the rather demanding requirements of the peacekeeping operations. But no other agreed compromise has yet been found to replace it.

NOTES

1. At least so far as General Assembly votes and even East European acquiescence in the Security Council are indicative of prevailing attitudes.

2. By comparison with the standard described on pages 24-25.

3. The United Nations authorized and administered several minor peacekeeping operations during 1947-63, including the following: UN Truce Supervision Organization in Palestine, UN Conciliation Commission for Palestine, UN Military Observer Group in India and Pakistan, UN Representative for India, UN Commission for the Unification and Rehabilitation of Korea, UN Observer Group in Lebanon, UN Presence in Laos. See Wainhouse et al. for detailed descriptions of functions, organization, and activities, and so on.

Budgeted expenditures for these operations, with few exceptions, amounted to approximately $2.5 to $4.5 million annually (1949, $5.4 million; 1958, $6.8 million), that is, to about 5 percent of the regular budget from which their funding was obtained.

The United Nations Temporary Executive Authority in West New Guinea active from October 1, 1962, to May 1963, involved expenditures of about $20 million of which less than one third was for peacekeeping. The Netherlands and Indonesia shared these expenses equally. Costs associated with the Yemen Observer Group active in 1963 were shared equally by Saudi Arabia and the United Arab Republic (Stoessinger et al., p. 105).

4. United Nations, General Assembly, *Official Records: Financial Report and*

Accounts for the Year Ended 31 December 1973, twenty-ninth session (New York, 1974). Hereinafter referred to as *Financial Report 1973.*

5. Includes $12 million of payments offered in nonconvertible currencies but excludes $16.6 million unpaid assessments on China that were transferred to a special account *(Financial Report 1973,* p. 141).

6. Several members had not responded to UNEF assessments for reserve requirements or for contributions to meet increased cost estimates. An additional thirty-four members were in arrears for UNEF, as were twenty-two members for ONUC. In total, sixty-two members were in arears for UNEF as were fifty-four members for ONUC.

7. UN General Assembly, *Official Records,* twenty-seventh session. Supplement 29 (A/8729).

8. Representatives of a number of developing countries nevertheless expressed strong objections to this proposal.

9. Cited by Wainhouse et al., p. 349.

10. Prospects at the time of writing are for a UN presence in Cyprus continuing indefinitely into the future.

11. Australia, Austria, Canada, Denmark, Finland, Ireland, New Zealand, Sweden, and the United Kingdom. For an exceedingly thorough account of their participation see Wainhouse et al., pp. 345-413.

12. Paradoxically, the largest financial contributor, the United States, also was the predominant source of unpaid pledges (UN General Assembly, *Official Records: Financial Report and Accounts for the Year Ended 31 December 1972* and *Report of the Board of Auditors,* twenty-eighth session, Suppl. 7 (A/9007).

13. Deprivation of voting rights in the Assembly.

14. Resolution 1739.

15. Several members that had adopted the view that UNEF and ONUC had generated "extraordinary expenses" subscribed to the bond issue notwithstanding. Many countries that had been in arrears on their peacekeeping assessments pledged to purchase bonds.

16. The judges were hardly unanimous on the issue. The majority opinion carried by a vote of 9 to 5, and the nationality of the judges seemed clearly associated with their positions (see Stoessinger et al., pp. 140 ff.).

17. See Russell, pp. 201-2.

18. A/Res. 2117 (XX), 12-21-65 (passed 44-14-46) and A/Res. 2194 (XXI), 12-16-66 (passed 56-11-25-30 [absent), cited in Russell, p. 347.

19. Larus, pp. 12 ff., provides an excellent account of the confused and acrimonious controversy surrounding the linking of Soviet, French, and American contributions.

20. Eventually the debate spread to conflict over the *size* of the deficit. See Larus, p. 9, and Table 2, above, for details.

21. The Soviet leadership, despite its devotion to long-term central planning and orderly interactions also held the basic solution to lie with ad hoc improvisations fitting the exigencies of the situation.

22. By 1975 the chief American delegate to the UN spoke of a "tyranny of the majority," to which the U.S. government was not about to submit.

23. Cited in Stoessinger et al., pp. 145-46.

24. Cited in Russell, p. 349.

25. Cited in Russell, p. 350.

26. Cited in Russell, p. 351.

27. The persistent efforts by the U.S. government to have its assessment reduced seems consistent with collective responsibility. Assessments regarded as inordinately high were accepted until constitutional means could be employed to obtain subsequent reductions. It might be argued, therefore, that the U.S. government was adhering to collective responsibility because it accepted implementation of existing rules even while working to obtain their modification.

28. It was not only in the UN where the ultimate mélange of ideologies clashed but also in presumably closely knit alliances with strong "common values and purposes" that finding an agreed basis for cost sharing was not solvable by simple references to collective responsibility. Even among members of a military-political alliance, "burden-sharing formulas are likely to be accepted only when the sums are relatively small and when the formulas offer no binding precedents for the future" (Pincus, p. 86). In the "realistic" world of international affairs dogged adherence to so unrealistic a principle as collective responsibility is interesting, to say the least.

29. This is perhaps nowhere more clearly demonstrated than when the Soviet representatives successfully resisted granting to individual members of the community permission to contribute directly and voluntarily to a UN peace fund (Brubaker, 1975b).

30. Bond sales might be regarded as still another major method, but unless the debt could be perpetually refinanced the essential problem of obtaining revenues for interest and amortization payments would have to be solved by some means to induce appropriate current financial flows. Thus, except under rather unlikely conditions bond sales would not permit escape from the basic problem. Furthermore, parties that refused financial support via current contributions might be expected to refuse purchase of bonds. And that, of course, is what they did. See page 61.

31. Involuntary contributions occur through organizational default when contributions in kind are made in unrealized anticipation of reimbursement.

32. Nonreimbursed claims for contributions to UNEF and ONUC amounted to $20 million and $10 million, respectively (Wainhouse et al., p. 575).

33. The nature of the problem is such, nevertheless, that closer approximation to efficient and equitable solutions are facilitated by simultaneous considerations of all relevant information.

34. One might argue that prior agreement on cost shares could eliminate the problem. But the impossibility of determining the pattern of benefit distribution for very far into the future under circumstances that were very difficult to foresee virtually precludes the possibility of obtaining a prior commitment by any sovereign decision maker to potentially major sacrifices in support of undesired activities.

35. If attention had been focused on the optimal level of the program rather than on enforcement of collective responsibility, decisions might have been reached to support more extensive programs.

CHAPTER VI

Voluntary Programs, Specialized Agencies, and International Nongovernmental Organizations

A. Voluntary Programs and Specialized Agencies

Intergovernmental cost sharing in the postwar period has, of course, not been limited to the programs described in the previous chapter. The special voluntary programs [1] administered through the UN's principal organs [2] and the programs of the specialized agencies [3] also have provided significant experience.

As the term implies, the special voluntary programs were financed primarily through contributions unilterally decided upon by national governments. Assessments were absent, but presumably inducements to contribute took other forms.

1. ASSESSMENTS VS. VOLUNTARY CONTRIBUTIONS

As we have seen, the distinction in practice between assessments and voluntary contributions probably is not nearly so sharp as their strict definitions seem to imply. Compare, for example, assessments with matching formulas. Matching formulas usually are associated with so-called voluntary arrangements. The United States, for instance, offered a formula for matching grants to UNICEF (Stoessinger et al., p. 193). The representatives of India and Japan made their contributions to the Expanded Programme of Technical Assistance and to the Special Fund [4] contingent upon matching by all others to meet a specified minimum (Stoessinger et al., p. 203). But it seems not at all farfetched to regard assessment scales as a multilateral matching mechanism, whereby the specifics of the matching are agreed within the Committee on Contributions. In the final analysis, national governmental representatives have the last word as to whether or not the suggested sacrifice will in fact be forthcoming. Thus, again, distinctions between voluntary contributions and assessments easily can be overemphasized.

The fiscal constitutional arrangements of the specialized agencies often resemble closely those for the regular budgets of the UN's principal organs. The arrangements emphasize collective responsibility. Many require a two-thirds majority on budgetary questions and permit suspension of voting rights as a sanction against certain financial delinquencies (Elmandjra, p. 214). As may be determined from inspecting Table 4, the predominant source of finance for these agencies has been assessed contributions. The assessment scales of the specialized agencies reflect the particular needs and circumstances of each, especially variations in membership, but by and large they turn out basically similar to that for the organization's regular budget.

The use by the specialized agencies of a mechanism similar to that of the principal organs has led to a basic problem similar to theirs. Namely, programs can be voted without adequate guarantees that the implied financial wherewithal subsequently will be forthcoming. Most of these agencies, including the ILO, WHO, ICAO, FAO, and others, have suffered from the problem of certain members falling seriously into arrears at one time or another (Stoessinger et al., pp. 219 ff.). Controversy has been relatively muted, however, apparently in part because membership in the specialized agencies has not been comprehensive, and in part because they have not been perceived so clearly as engaged in programs with definitely negative outputs for specific governments.

2. ATTEMPTS AT NOVEL SOLUTIONS

Authorities responsible for dealing with financial problems of the specialized agencies and the voluntary programs sometimes have attempted novel solutions that seem to have escaped the attention of those facing similar problems related to the regular budget. For example, officials of the Universal Postal Union (UPU) and the International Telecommunication Union (ITU) have instituted interest charges on members' arrears (Stoessinger et al., p. 234). Attempts have been made to relate assessments to benefits. The ICAO bases its scale in part on the interest in, and importance of, civil aviation in the various member countries. The UPU assessments have been a function of population, area, and the volume of postal traffic (Pincus, p. 92). The IMCO considers the tonnage of the merchant fleets of its members (Elmandjra, p. 233). In spite of such efforts, however, the main criterion seems to have been simple

TABLE 4

UNITED NATIONS EXPENDITURES BY SOURCE OF FUNDS[a]
(MILLIONS OF CURRENT U.S. DOLLARS)

	1947	1949	1951	1953	1955	1957	1959	1961	1963	1965	1967	1969	1970
Assessed													
Administered under:													
Principal Organs	27	43	49	49	50	53	62	71	92	107	130	157	168
Specialized Agencies	19	28	30	33	37	44	61	72	100	139	174	212	232
Total[b]	46	70	78	82	87	97	122	143	192	246	305	369	401
Voluntary													
Administered under:													
Principal Organs	1	86	71	65	74	108	96	120	171	204	271	353	374
Specialized Agencies		2	1	2	2	2	6	9	6	14	8	12	13
Total[b]	1	88	72	67	75	110	102	129	177	218	279	365	387

[a] Adapted from Elmandjra, pp. 228-31. Data exclude expenditures for: peacekeeping, the Korean Reconstruction Agency (UNKRA), Relief for Hungarian Refugees (UNRHR), and the specialized trust funds.

[b] Components may not sum to total because of rounding.

ability to pay. Faced with cases of persistent arrears, the WHO and UNESCO kept two budgets—one based on assessments of active and inactive members and a second, "effective working budget," based on assessments of active members only (Stoessinger et al., pp. 221, 229). Consequently these agencies were able to avoid a cumulating deficit. Another tactic employed, apparently to good advantage, by the ILO was to "remain undercommitted" (Stoessinger et al., p. 220). Perhaps most interesting of all, a voluntary program, UNICEF, has employed a matching formula according to which the governments of assisted countries arrange transfers of $2.00 to $2.50 for every $1.00 transferred through UNICEF (Stoessinger et al., p. 195). It would appear that measures similar to the above could be adapted to facilitate resolution of the problems that have proved so damaging to the financial operations under the principal organs.

B. International Nongovernmental Organizations

1. DEFINITION

Still another variety of international cost-sharing experience, that of international nongovernmental organizations (INGOs), provides valuable insight into the general phenomenon. INGOs are distinguished by great diversity and spontaneity reflecting individual initiative to meet needs of diverse and geographically isolated memberships. They range from widely known and large organizations like the International Red Cross to those smaller and less prominent such as the Associated Country Women of the World or the International Goat Breeding Federation. Precise definition of the boundaries defining the set of INGOs has been especially difficult.[5] The frequently quoted definition employed by the UN's Economic and Social Council—"any international organization which is not established by intergovernmental agreement,"—would seem to encompass a broad range of organizations engaged in the production of private goods and services for profit, the multinational corporations. Of special interest here, however, are those INGOs engaged in creating goods and services associated with substantial amounts of the collective-good properties. Thus, our focus excludes the famous multinational corporations or any other commercially oriented business enterprise, no matter how wide the geographic range of its activities.

2. ECONOMIC SIGNIFICANCE

Data in Table 5 on budgets of INGOs provide at least an indication of the lower limit to the economic significance of their activities. The data would seem to constitute a lower limit, because they were obtained from a survey to which there was no response from a large percentage of organizations solicited, and probably more important, services of volunteers presumably usually were not included in the budget. Even so, the totals show that the economic scope of INGOs from the early 1950s to the mid-1960s was appreciable by comparision with the budgets of the United Nations system.

TABLE 5
BUDGETS OF RESPONDING INGOS, 1951-64[a]

Budget (Million Current Dollars)			Number of Respondents	
Year	Total	Average	Units	Percent of Total Solicited
1951	42.2	.134	315	38
1954	232.2	.710	327	32
1958	291.0	.610	477	45
1960	305.8	.587	521	42
1964	262.3	.629	417	28

[a] *Yearbook of International Organizations,* 15th ed. (1971), p. 535.

Some feeling for the type of activites engaged in, the potential for creating globally collective goods, and the means employed to generate revenues might be gained by examining information presented in Table 6 on objectives, activities, and modes for finance of some prominent INGOs. Of particular interest here is the fact that at least some of their activities result in essentially globally shared goods, principally income transfers and development aid, and promotion of basic knowledge. Other activites involve sharing on a rather more limited basis. But in this respect they differ little from activities of governments and purely commercial entities that often also range widely in terms of creating some purely private goods and some goods associated with substantial externalities. For analytical purposes, it would be very useful to separate activities according to the private-collective character of the goods created and to possess accurate measures of the full extent and distribution of the benefits created by them. In fact, the data probably reflect much more closely, however inaccurately and ambiguously, merely their aggregate resource costs. Unsuitable as they are for present purposes, the data nevertheless, do indicate a very rough order of magnitude for the economic significance of these activites.

Approximately 10 percent of INGOs have on occasion been subsi-

TABLE 6

OBJECTIVES, ACTIVITIES, AND MODES OF FINANCE OF SELECTED PROMINENT INGO'S

Organization	Objectives and Activities	Modes of Finance
Cooperative for American Relief Everywhere (CARE)	Provide on a people-to-people basis food and self-help assistance including tools and materials for agriculture, education, health and social services, family planning, and nutritional education. Staff: United States 255 United States-Canadian Overseas 131 Indigenous 880	Contributions by individuals, civic groups, philanthropic and business organizations primarily in the US and Canada. Supplements obtained via cost-shared partnership agreements with host governments. Donations totaled $31,930,269 in the fiscal year ended June 30, 1975 of which almost $18 million was in cash and almost $14 million was in kind. Services donated are not included because of difficulty in determining their value.[a]
Coordinating Board of Jewish Organizations	Coordinate work at the United Nations of three constituent organizations [b] promoting human rights and combating persecution or discrimination on grounds of race, religion, or origin.	Contributions by constituent bodies whose total annual budget is $16,000,000.

TABLE 6

OBJECTIVES, ACTIVITIES, AND MODES OF FINANCE OF SELECTED PROMINENT INGO'S

Organization	Objectives and Activities	Modes of Finance
International Chamber of Commerce	Represent international business, including commerce, industry, transport, and finance. Secure effective and consistent action for improvement of business conditions between nations and for solution of international economic problems. Encourage communication between businessmen in various countries. Court of International Arbitration established to enable quick settlement of disputes of businessmen from different countries. International Council on Advertising Practice settles claims of alleged unfair competition in international advertising.	Contributions by national committees according to "economic importance" of countries. Budget for 1972 was $680,000.
International Council of Scientific Unions	Coordinate and facilitate activities of international scientific unions in the natural sciences. Maintain relations with national governments and the United Nations to promote science.	Member dues. Grants from UNESCO. Voluntary contributions.

Organization	Objectives and Activities	Modes of Finance
International Red Cross	Care for casualties of war. Aid prisoners and other victims of hostilities. Relief of suffering in peacetime including disaster relief, first aid, and preventive medicine. Other activities covering many aspects of health and welfare. Since 1919 the League of Red Cross Societies coordinated more than 320 emergency relief operations. In a ten year period from the mid-1960s to the mid-1970s it initiated 150 appeals via national societies. Membership 225,000,000 adults and juniors in 116 countries.	Contributions of member societies to the League of Red Cross Societies are on a "prorata" basis. Total budget 1973 was 5.1 million Swiss francs. Value of relief in cash and kind in a recent decade—640 million Swiss francs.
International Union for Child Welfare	Spread principles of Declaration of Rights of children. Relief for children in distress. Contribute to physical and moral development of children and youth.	Member's dues. Contributions. Bequests. Interest from investments. Grants. Sale of publications. Administrative budget for 1972 was 1.4 million Swiss francs.

SOURCE: *Yearbook of International Organizations*, 15th ed., 1974.

[a] CARE, Inc., 29th Annual Report, 1975.

[b] B'nai B'rith (members in Canada, United States, and 42 other countries); Board of Deputies of British Jews; South African Jewish Board of Deputies. Combined membership 930,000 in 44 countries.

dized by grants from governments, but subsidies often have been looked upon with great disfavor by association managements concerned about the potential for dependence. Those INGOs engaged primarily in creating close approximations to purely collective goods must rely essentially on contributions from interested individuals. They may be members of an association paying dues or responding to assessments. They may be nonmembers responding to a solicitation. In any event, the distinguishing feature is the essentially voluntary nature of the individual's decisions, although some social pressure may be applied. Advertisements may employ psychologically powerful inducement. "Fair shares" may be indicated. Matching formulas may be proposed. Nevertheless, for the argument of this book the most salient fact about INGOs is that very sizable programs, sometimes essentially global, with important collective-good elements, have in fact been supported largely on the basis of voluntary contributions from individual human beings.

NOTES

1. United Nations Relief and Works Agency for Palestine Refugees in the Near East (UNRWA), United Nations High Commissioner for Refugee (UNHCR), United Nations Conference on Trade and Development (UNCTAD), United Nations Development Programme (UNDP), United Nations Industrial Development Organization (UNIDO), United Nations Institute for Training and Research (UNITAR), United Nations Children's Fund (UNICEF).

2. The General Assembly, the Security Council, Economic and Social Council, the Trusteeship Council, the International Court of Justice, and the Secretariat.

3. International Labor Organization (ILO), Food and Agriculture Organization (FAO), United Nations Educational, Scientific, and Cultural Organization (UNESCO), World Health Organization (WHO), International Monetary Fund (IMF), International Development Association (IDA), International Bank for Reconstruction and Development (IBRD), International Finance Corporation (IFC), International Civil Aviation Organization (ICAO), World Meteorological Organization (WMO), Intergovernmental Maritime Consultative Organization (IMCO).

4. For information on the Special Fund and its relationship with other organizations, see Elmandjra, pp. 58 ff.

5. See Skjelsbaek (1971) for an extended discussion.

CHAPTER VII

Individual Values and International Security Programs: Evidence

The debate over international cost sharing, while rife with confused controversy, indicates at least some perception of need for joint programs. But little is known about the extent and intensity of such perceptions. From the microtheoretic perspective, another highly relevant question needs to be directly and thoroughly addressed: What basis already exists for judging latent demand for international security programs?

A. Purpose

As noted at the outset, casual impressions suggest a rather intense and widespread desire for law, order, and justice in the international community. Clearly, this desire is not universally overriding, but it does seem to be the predominant preference pattern. Substantial economic resources are allocated worldwide to orderly pursuit of justice at various levels of social organization. National security expenditures have been described with increasing frequency by their administrators as directed toward maintenance of "peace," that is, international law and order. The purpose of the present chapter is to explore some issues pertinent to inferences about the extent and intensity of latent demand for international security programs.

The discussion will, of course, rely conceptually on the framework developed in Chapter III, and in this context a number of very interesting questions arise. Has the relatively low level of de facto expression of demand resulted from inexorable operation of the general laws of collective economic action? Is it an empirical verification of behavior predicted by orthodox Western economic theory? Or is the apparently low level of demand the result rather of institutionalized outright prohibition of economic expression of individual values?

B. Conceptions of Product

In any study of demand it is useful to be able to specify clearly the good. In the present case we must acknowledge that the specification will vary from time to time and from circumstance to circumstance and in each instance will remain more or less vague. One useful approach may entail, therefore, timely description by IO administrators of programs they judge appropriate for a certain period. The administrators will not be able to guarantee the precise nature of the activities, let alone their outcomes. The expectations of individuals regarding outcomes will vary in accordance with their judgments about the mechanisms underlying operation of the international system, about the impact of past activities, and about alternative analytical models for projecting future impacts.

There may be considerable concern about the high degree of uncertainty necessarily associated with an international organization's security programs and especially with our imprecise understanding of their effects. We need not despair, however, over the unavoidable obstacles to a precise definition of the product. Such obstacles are hardly peculiar to peacekeeping and peacemaking activities. It is not at all obvious that other international collective goods can be defined with any greater precision. Nor is it the property of internationality that is the source of difficulty. Collective goods at lower levels of social organization—national defense; education; law, order, and the administration of justice, for instance—also more often than not are scarcely any less nebulous notions. Indeed, lack of knowledge about the actual effects of the consumption activity is a problem shared by many private goods such as medical services, which unavoidably also often incorporate risk of disaster. Despite the uncertainty individuals may feel about the precise nature of such goods, and despite their aversion to risk, the expected utility seems sufficient to elicit a considerable expression of demand. It is entirely possible, even likely, that despite the grave uncertainties inhering in any peacekeeping and peacemaking program of an international organization, there may exist a similarly considerable latent demand.

Evaluation of the impact of alternative programs that might be proposed by administrators of an international organization and comparison of the costs and benefits of such programs with alternative potential uses of resources [1] is beyond the scope of this work. Assessment of programs, in any event, probably will vary greatly among individuals, including the most sophisticated and capable of scholars.[2] No doubt some individuals would find the proposed activities to be worthless, if not worse, and, of course their monetary evaluation would be set accordingly. Others may find the programs to be of substantial value. It is not our purpose to evaluate the merits of such views. It is simply to provide and interpret evidence regarding their extent and intensity, an apparently comparatively modest goal, although it may be regarded as no less than monumental by some.

Like programs for seeking law, order, and justice at lower levels of social organization, IOPOPJ appear to constitute an example par excellence of a collective good. The benefit from IOPOPJ to any one individual, whatever it might be, would not be diminished by its extension to an additional person. The benefit could not be denied to anyone who maintained that IOPOPJ were worth nothing to him and who consequently refused to pay. Clearly, the ultimate in large groups is involved. It would seem, therefore, that the accumulated wisdom regarding the general character of such goods and the behavior of individuals when asked for an expression of demand for them should be highly relevant.

Specifically, the currently dominant strain of neoclassical orthodoxy suggests that the free-rider hypothesis would be applicable, so the individual monetary evaluations would not be revealed, and therefore, finances for IOPOPJ could not be obtained without taxation. For reasons elaborated in Chpater III, this is certainly a possibility to be reckoned with, but it is not a complete picture or even a dependable outline of reality. There are important circumstances in which free-rider behavior seems far from overwhelming. The existence of collective-good-creating INGOs such as the International Red Cross and CARE may be cited as evidence. "Superficially selfless actions," observed repeatedly to accompany external disasters,[3] may be relevant to judging individual willingness to reveal demand for IOPOPJ, since the operation of the international system periodically has created notable, to say the least, disasters. More subtle but persistent calamities also may evoke in some a willingness to gamble on IOPOPJ. Consider, for example, expenditures for various national security programs that roughly equal the total income of the poorer half of all mankind and that may tend to produce as much or more trepidation abroad as security at home. Finally, the evidence to be presented below also points clearly in the direction of substantial latent demand for IOPOPJ and some potential for its revelation.

C. Factors Affecting Demand for International Security Programs

Before examining that evidence, it may be useful to consider some qualitative factors relevant specifically to latent and revealed demand for international security programs.

1. PROHIBITION OF ECONOMIC EXPRESSIONS OF DEMAND

While revelations of demand under individual voluntarism may be incomplete, they may, nevertheless, significantly exceed those that have occurred in response to previously existing institutions. The most prominent international organizations, the UN in particular, far from being allowed to tax, quite to the contrary have been *prohibited* from performing vital intermediation services, that is, from accepting purely voluntary expressions of economic demand for IOPOPJ directly from private individuals and organizations. Certain persons opposed to particular international security programs have not been willing to allow the allegedly natural tendency to ride free to lead automatically to the atrophy of IOPOPJ, but have felt necessary not merely the refusal to contribute themselves but also the institutionalization of outright prohibition of contributions by others. It seems quite likely that the fact that individuals have contributed nothing at all directly to IOPOPJ in the past has far less to do with the universality of free-riding than with the fact the UN executives have never asked for a disclosure of demand.[4] And in turn they have never asked because they have been prohibited [5] by national officials from doing so. The essential point is that the extent of demand expressed for any collective need may be affected decisively by the existence of a respected intermediary. Without one, a very large potential demand may remain latent.

The propensity to donate probably would vary with the degree of overt international conflict and with apprehensions about its imminence. During periods of open warfare, even if local, with all of its tangible and intangible costs, revealed demand probably would tend to be high. Similarly, during periods of heavy national military expenditure, that is, during an arms race, the need for an alternative may be especially strongly felt.

2. PERCEPTION OF NEED

Differences in perception of need for IOPOPJ relative to other collective needs such as public health, or other public investment for economic development, plausibly may be regarded as a source of variation of latent and revealed demand. An individual's decision may be influenced by his opinions about his nation's interest as well as by the extent to which he feels personally threatened by existing or potential international disorder. He may consider also the extent to which his own profession and perhaps his own career in a national governmental establishment may be affected by IOPOPJ.

Volatility in perception of need seems highly probable. Because the intensity of conflict, itself often volatile, may be expected to influence demand for IOPOPJ, one might anticipate considerable corresponding fluctuation in revelation of demand. Furthermore, decisions of the IO executive in a situation of ongoing conflict are likely to provoke sudden changes in attitude and, accordingly, in the propensity to donate.[6] Finally, those (individuals or governments) who go through a period of apprehension that they are about to become victims of lawlessness and disorder may experience a profound rise in their preference for IOPOPJ relative to other goods.[7]

3. PERCEPTION OF EFFECTIVENESS

An individual's latent demand probably will be influenced by his perception of efficiency and effectiveness. If international organizational activities are regarded as having attained their objectives or as having laid a plausible foundation for future programs, individuals are more likely to continue to contribute. Substantiated charges of waste and corruption almost certainly would result in a tendency toward a reduced flow of voluntary donations as well as in requests for changes in administrators. Consequently, some funds undoubtedly will find their way to a public relations department to "explain" the organization's programs. As a balance, however, the independent press, academic circles, and national governments will have ample opportunity to present their independent evaluations of performance.

4. PARTICIPATION IN DECISIONS

The intensity of an individual's demand as well as his willingness to reveal it may vary directly with the extent of participation in major decisions, principally choice of a chief administrator. Alternatively, one might suppose that any of a large number of possible administrative mechanisms that were judged to be reasonably effective, impartial, and free of corruptibility would be regarded with indifference by private donors whose main concern is securing the benefits of international order. They may feel, too, that inasmuch as they have discretion over whether to contribute to financing the administrator's proposed programs the choice of individuals for the post is somewhat less vital.

An especially delicate aspect of perception of effectiveness involves impartiality of administration. Where an individual donor's personal in-

terests, including those of his local community, are only remotely involved, if at all, he presumably will prefer impartial administration of
IOPOPJ and will assess performance in some degree according to this
criterion. Perfect impartiality, difficult to define, probably attainable only
with the best of good fortune, and likely to be misinterpreted by some
even if attained, would constitute a challenging objective for the IO
administrator.

5. ELITE ATTITUDES

Individual latent and revealed demands undoubtedly will be affected
significantly by national officials, both through their setting of ground
rules for individual contributions and through their persuasive efforts
thereafter. Complex interactions between officials and other individuals
seem inevitable. On the one hand, leaders reflect, however imperfectly,
the views of individuals in the society. But on the other, national officials
have been comparatively active in the field of foreign relations, consti-
tuting a major source of pertinent factual knowledge and, therefore,
especially in this area have formed views as well as reflected them. Furthermore, leadership leverage in setting ground rules can be decisive at
the very outset. Refusal by a single powerful regime to permit individual
economic expressions of demand may suffice to prevent them *everywhere*. In this respect, the impact of its refusal upon persons well outside
its nominal jurisdiction can be quite remarkable. Doubtlessly more subtle rules also can have important even if less overwhelming effects.

D. Evidence

With these considerations in mind, let us examine the evidence from
which we might draw some inferences, or at least indications, about the
extent both of latent demand for IOPOPJ and of the degree to which it
might be revealed.

1. INDIVIDUAL SPECULATION

Several authorities on international organization have expressed notions about the possible extent of voluntary contributions to a UN peace
and security fund open to private individuals and organizations. Given
the great inherent uncertainties and the lack of experience with such a
fund, it is hardly surprising that there is a rather wide divergence of
opinion.

Undoubtedly, one of the more optimistic [8] assertions was made by
Lincoln P. Bloomfield when in 1962 he wrote in a letter to the *New York
Times* that "if there were a world-wide appeal for . . . a UN endowment,

subscriptions in excess of one billion dollars would be realized from individuals, foundations, governments and private corporations." He cited "the urge of men everywhere to make a personal contribution to a meaningful cause."

John G. Stoessinger et al. and Norman J. Padelford (10-26-62) have commented that few analysts have been so optimistic about the total contribution that might be forthcoming. They cite the lethargic response to UN bond sales and limited gifts of individuals, groups, and foundations in the past. It might be noted, however, that past experience involved only funds for activities other than international security and no attempt to guarantee a minimum level of results and, therefore, may not be indicative of the extent of potential revelation of demand for IOPOPJ. By the 1970s populations and per capita nominal incomes have risen to the extent that the required average annual $0.25 per person contribution necessary for a $1 billion flow would not seem wildly unrealistic.[9]

Joel Larus, while suggesting that "there appears to be little hope of achieving agreement on a pre-arranged plan paying costs of a future UN force," proposed an Anniversary Fund drive to take place during 1969-70 with the limited purpose essentially of eliminating UN debts (p. 1). Larus thought that a feasible target for the drive would be $258 million—an amount somewhat more than sufficient to liquidate the accounts outstanding for the United Nations Emergency Force and the United Nations Congo Operation and to pay the remaining principal on the UN bond issue (pp. 20-21). Larus did not argue that this target is the maximum that might be achieved, but that it is a limited goal that the national governments might find tolerable.

In sum, careful analysts of international organization and its financing have been duly wary in estimating the size of a peace and security fund that might accumulate in response to an appeal to a wide variety of possible sources of support including private individuals and organizations. Even so, the differences of opinion are striking. Padelford states that "it hardly seems likely that non-governmental contributions will in the foreseeable future approach the point of displacing member state payments for any of the normal operations of the Organization or for . . . maintaining peace and order" (10-26-62, p. 21). Bloomfield and Larus, on the other hand, apparently feel that sums of several hundred million or even a billion dollars may not be beyond the realm of reasonable expectations. On one thing everyone can agree: in the present state of knowledge a great deal of confidence in any estimate is hardly appropriate.

In order to provide a firmer foundation for judgments similar to those cited and in order to evaluate trends in individual values regarding IOPOPJ, assembly and interpretation of currently available relevant evidence would seem highly useful. Such evidence appears indirect and meager, but what is available tends to reinforce the casual observation that the potential effective aggregate demand for IOPOPJ may amount to a considerable sum. The current evidence suggests both that latent demand may be substantial and that significant absolute amounts may be revealed. The indications include attempts at unsolicited contributions, governmental financial support for UN peacekeeping operations, public opinion polls, and statements by governmental representatives.

2. UNSOLICITED PRIVATE OFFERS

First of all, private individuals and groups have sought to make *unsolicited* contributions to the UN (Stoessinger et al., pp. 256 ff.). According to Stoessinger et al., "Some of these private efforts have shown originality and demonstrated considerable persistence over the years." There also have been attempts to pass legislation to permit private purchase of UN bonds and to make contributions to the UN deductible for U.S. federal income tax purposes.[10]

Evidence of economic expression of individual desires to contribute to control international violence is not confined to the United States. The Soviet government newspaper, *Izvestia,* of January 29, 1972, reported that "the Patriarchate of Moscow has contributed 3,000,000 rubles to the Soviet Peace Fund . . ." and that "In his letter to the Board of the Soviet Peace Fund [the] Patriarch . . . said: 'We sincerely wish that this money, together with other contributions to the fund from public organizations and private individuals, will help to maintain peace on earth.' " Granting that the Soviet Peace Fund and a UN peace and security fund may not be quite the same, this apparent expression of willingness of individual Soviet citizens to contribute material resources seems indicative of the breadth of existence of individual desires for international order. Indeed, a more systematic study covering a larger number of medium and high per capita income countries may be worthwhile.

3. FINANCIAL SUPPORT THROUGH NATIONAL GOVERNMENTS

An examination of the sources of finance for past United Nations peacekeeping operations may provide some clues about the extent and distribution of demand for certain IOPOPJ. A detailed study by David Wainhouse and his associates shows that the UN had reported budgetary expenditures of almost $800 million for nine selected peacekeeping operations during the period from May 1948 to December 1968.[11] Four of the decidedly less expensive operations, peace observation missions, were financed under the regular UN budget. Thus, in effect they were supported by *all* member states [12] with the exception of a few years (1963-67) when the USSR and associated countries refused to accept a share of their assessments attributable to the United Nations Truce Supervision Organization.

Special accounts (outside the regular budget) were created to provide financing for the UNEF and the ONUC. Over half of UN member governments have failed to pay as scheduled their assessed contributions for these accounts; and as we have seen in Chapter V, refusal to pay by a number of governments, notably the French and the Soviet, contributed to a general UN "crisis," which as of the late 1970's promised to drag on indefinitely. Voluntary contributions by governments have constituted the means of financing the United Nations Force in Cyprus, and they have added to funds for UNEF and ONUC. If one includes member countries that purchased UN bonds, well over half have provided support in addition to assessments. Furthermore, many countries provided direct material support for which they were not reimbursed; and finally, some nations incurred considerable costs for which they never asked reimbursement. [13]

The operations took place in diverse parts of the world under a variety of circumstances and took a variety of forms. Thus, the expression of willingness to pay for international peacekeeping was a response of governments to concrete conflict situations that each interpreted and responded to, perhaps more from a sense of immediate impact on its relative international position than from a desire to honor an abstract commitment to restraint of international violence. Given the circumstances under which contributions (including "assessments") have been made, and given the complexity of contributors' motives and of their relation to individual preferences, it seems doubtful, to say the least, that the historical record on governmental contributions to international peacekeeping activities will contribute much more than slight hints as to the general public's willingness to contribute financially to peace and security operations of international organizations. It does seem significant, nevertheless, that on occasion all member states, whether enthusiastically or not, actually have contributed to specialized international peacekeeping services.

4. OPINION POLLS

The results of a Gallup poll taken in the United States in early October 1970 are consistent with existence of a substantial latent demand for international security programs. The poll posed two questions. First: "It has been suggested that the United Nations establish a peacekeeping army of about 100,000 men. Do you favor or oppose such a plan?" There is no indication that interviewees were asked to contemplate the financial implications of their response, but for interpreting the results it may be of interest to provide a crude first approximation to the implied level of expenditure. According to data in the Stockholm International Peace Research Institute's *Yearbook of World Armaments and Disarmament 1969/70* (pp. 273, 276) in 1969 with about 3.5 million persons in the armed services, officially estimated military expenditures in the United States amounted to $80 billion, that is, to about $2 billion per 100,000 men. Thus, even after allowing for the high expenditure per man in the United States relative to other countries, the question stated in the poll clearly is asking indirectly about the respondent's opinion on the desirability of what might very well turn out to be a substantial expenditure for peacekeeping services. It is true, of course, that questions focusing the interviewee's attention on the potential benefit while disregarding the cost, and his share of it, may lead to responses creating an exaggerated impression of willingness to contribute. The responses do, nevertheless, provide some relevant evidence. Persons opposing the plan even if others paid the bill could hardly be expected to make a contribution. A statement in its favor at least leaves open the possibility of willingness to reveal some monetary evaluation. According to the reported results of the poll, 64 percent responded in favor, 22 percent were opposed, and 14 percent had no opinion.[14] The response to the more general question, "Would you like to see the United Nations become a stronger organization?" was even more emphatic. Eighty-four percent of the respondents answered yes, 8 percent no, and 8 percent no opinion.[15]

Similar results were reported from a Gallup survey of statesmen, scientists, educators, and other leaders from seventy noncommunist countries *(New York Times,* September 29, 1973, p. 2). To the question, "Would you like to have the United Nations become a stronger organization or not?" 81 percent responded yes, 14 percent no, and 5 percent no opinion. Great caution in interpreting these results seems warranted, but they also seem to suggest that the existence of a substantial and widespread effective demand for international peacekeeping services cannot be ruled out and that a more direct investigation of the intensity of demand may be worthwhile.

5. NATIONAL OFFICIALS' DECLARATIONS ABOUT A UN PEACE AND SECURITY FUND

Perhaps the most direct evidence on virtually *worldwide* attitudes toward a UN peace and security fund per se may be found in official statements by the various national governmental representatives to the organization. Clues about the general public's demand for international organizational peacekeeping and peacemaking operations may be sought in the record on governmental attitudes toward such a fund.

As far as can be determined from the documentary evidence, the overwhelming majority of member governments, at one time or another, have expressed approval of, or willingness to tolerate, contributions to a peacekeeping fund from individuals or nongovernmental organizations.[16] Thus, in 1961 when the possibility of a fund open to nongovernmental contributions was discussed by the Working Group of 15,[17] representatives of seven member states [18] supported it. Three [19] opposed it, and five [20] took no definite position (UN Doc. A/4971). At the fourth special session of the General Assembly representatives of the governments of Cyprus, Ghana, the Ivory Coast, and Nigeria proposed study of the desirability and feasibility of establishing a peace fund, and on June 27, 1963, the General Assembly adopted by a vote of 91 to 12, with 2 abstentions, a resolution (18-79, S-IV) calling for the secretary general to solicit from all UN members and other interested organizations their ideas on a peace fund (UN Doc. A/5490).

Of the fifty-one member states that communicated their observations, thirty-four [21] supported or acquiesced in permitting private contributions. Seven [22] were opposed, and ten [23] reserved opinion pending further study. Outside of the Soviet government along with its constituent republics and its Eastern European allies, only the Central African Republic opposed the plan, but rich industrial nations including the United States were prominent among those expressing some reservations and desire for further study.

On the whole, however, governmental support seems overwhelming. In fact, among the ten governments reserving opinion, those of Italy, Japan, and the United States, had previously supported the idea when it was discussed in the Working Group of 15.[24] It seems doubtful that the governments of the remainder [25] would have objected so strenuously as to prohibit individual contributions from private citizens and organizations in their countries if and when a fund were established.

Again, circumspection seems especially appropriate when making inferences about the state of individual values from any particular set of assertions by a sample of officials. Nevertheless, the overwhelming General Assembly vote for study of the fund and the solid support expressed in the submissions of member states clearly point toward existence of significant potential demand for IOPOPJ.

The evidence, reflecting the scant resources allocated to its collection, the ban on individual contributions, and the modest efforts at collective-good intermediation by the United Nations organization, is much more meager than might be desired. Nevertheless, in the context of objectively and incontrovertibly enormous and growing global interdependence, it does provide sufficient indications of a potentially vast latent demand to warrant far more extensive and intensive exploration.

NOTES

1. Issues related to a broadly construed cost-benefit analysis of voluntary private contributions to IOPOPJ will be addressed in Chapter VIII, below.

2. There may be conditions under which distinction between peacekeeping and warmaking may be be difficult and subjective. This does not, of course, rule out the possibility that some peacekeeping programs may enjoy very widespread recognition as instrumental to order beneficial to virtually all.

3. Christopher Douty has provided an intriguing account and analysis.

4. It might be asked whether the UN has a monopoly on the potential for international peacekeeping or whether it might just as well be done by CARE, the RED Cross, and the like. We may tend at first to think of peacekeeping as a natural monopoly at any level of society. But peacekeeping clearly is a complex and relatively little understood art, sometimes with important roles for many participants. At the global level officials of nongovernmental organizations, national governments, and international organizations may have parts to play. Establishment of a complete set of guidelines for determining an appropriate distribution of roles seems likely to be a rather ambitious task. The thesis of this book does, however, have at least one important relevant implication. Specifically, even individuals may plausibly participate rather directly in a rather important phase of the process, namely, deciding about how much support to provide to potentially active peacekeepers. People can participate by expressing through the most effective means usually at their disposal, contributions of their wealth, to support those programs in which they perceive the greatest expected value. They may wish to support several simultaneously. The disparate roles decreed by rules of the game in the recent past are rather interesting, to say the least. Individuals have been compelled to support national governments. They have *generally* been free to support nongovernmental organizations but prohibited from supporting UN peacekeeping efforts.

5. Prohibition of contributions clearly has no basis whatsoever in the general economic principles of sharing. The broader case for and against it is examined in Chapter VIII.

6. Individual citizens probably contribute willingly to support lower-level law enforcement under the assumption that they themselves will be in no need of constraint by the authorities. At the time of arrest, an individual's demand for such services may drop drastically.

7. Excluding demand for national security programs that may rise even more rapidly.

8. Relative to other commentators. No judgment is expressed here regarding

its accuracy. For all we know, the estimate may have been an understatement of the latent demand.

9. Twenty-five cent per person seems like a rather modest average amount to ask of individuals in the high-income countries. Even in some of the lowest-income countries it would not seem an inordinate request. Indian and Chinese military expenditures per capita in the late 1960s appear to have amounted, very roughly, to $3 and $10 per year, respectively. Presumably, international peace-keeping and peacemaking operations would substitute to some extent for national military expenditure.

10. For a more recent attempt along similar lines, see H. R. 7053, "A Bill to amend the Internal Revenue Code of 1954 to provide that "a taxpayer conscientiously opposed to participation in war may elect to have his income, estate, or gift tax payments spent for nonmilitary purposes; to create a trust fund (the World Peace Tax Fund) to receive these tax payments . . ." (93d Cong. lst sess., April 16, 1973).

11. The method of aggregation is necessarily quite crude. For example, expenditures for various periods appear to have been summed with no adjustment for changes in the general level of prices from one year to the next.

12. For thorough discussions of factors affecting the size of governmental contributions see Wainhouse et al., chap. 4, and Stoessinger et al.

13. A notable exception to its legendary opposition was the Soviet Union's airlift of soldiers and supplies at the outset of the UN Congo Operation (Wainhouse et al., p. 137).

14. The poll also reported responses of persons in subsets according to attributes such as race, sex, education, age, income and so on.

15. Eighty-six to 89 percent of those with incomes of $10,000 or more answered yes.

16. At the somewhat more abstract level of public general declarations (lip service?) there appears to be a remarkable consensus, in fact virtual unanimity, on the need for strengthening the UN. For one noteworthy example see the joint communiqué issued in Moscow on May 29, 1972, by Soviet and American governmental leaders.

17. Working Group of 15 on the Examination of the Administrative and Budgetary Procedures of the UN established by General Assembly resolution 1620 (XV) of 21 April 1961.

18. France, Italy, Japan, Nigeria, Sweden, the United Arab Republic, and the United States.

19. Bulgaria, the USSR, and the United Kingdom.

20. Brazil, Canada, Republic of China, India, and Mexico.

21. Argentina, Ceylon, Republic of China, Columbia, Cyprus, Denmark, Dominican Republic, India, Jamaica, Liberia, Norway, Rwanda, Sudan, Sweden, Togo, Turkey, Uganda, United Kingdom of Great Britain and Northern Ireland, Venezuela, Afghanistan, Chad, Ecuador, Ghana, Indonesia, Brazil, Congo (Brazzaville), Iceland, Iran, Spain, Philippines, Upper Volta, Nepal, Congo (Leopoldville), and Nigeria.

22. USSR, Byelorussian Soviet Socialist Republic, Ukrainian Soviet Socialist Republic, Czechoslovakia, Hungary, Bulgaria, and the Central African Republic.

23. Canada, Chile, Italy, Japan, Netherlands, Australia, New Zealand, Cambodia, Syria, and the United States.

24. In 1971 the report of a presidential commission stated, "a public drive to solicit private contributions to the UN would be most appropriate and feasible." *Report of the President's Commission for the Observance of the Twenty-fifth Anniversary of the United Nations* (Washington, D.C.: Government Printing Office, 1971), p. 47.

25. Canada, Chile, the Netherlands, Australia, New Zealand, Cambodia, and Syria.

CHAPTER VIII

Proposals for Reform

The great significance and glaring deficiencies of the UN's financial mechanisms for eliciting whatever latent demand that may exist inevitably provoked numerous proposals for reform. Such proposals have been aimed at manifest, and often very specific deficiencies, mainly the deficit and undependability of revenue sources. Equity and efficiency have been only implicit objectives, and, understandably, no coherent strategy for attaining them has been formulated. Before submitting our own proposals based on the foregoing review and analysis, it will be useful to summarize and comment upon some of the prominent previous suggestions.[1] Many proposals are simply quite specific modifications of the UN's regular assessment scale designed to achieve compromises in concrete situations. Our purpose here is to focus on proposals embodying new principles rather than to evaluate or propose specific scales, each applicable to a particular set of circumstances but probably not to any other.

A. Alternative Revenue Sources

Failure of the UN's revenues to meet its expenses apparently has prompted some analysts to emphasize alternative sources, procedures, and mechanisms for obtaining revenue. Such sources include earmarked national taxes, voluntary governmental contributions, voluntary contributions from nongovernmental decision makers, and levies on specific transnational transactions. Let's consider each in turn.

The most prominent and probably predominant mechanism [2] for arranging for allocation of resources to production of collective goods at the national and lower levels of organization is delegation of authority to a small set of individuals both for expenditure decisions and for collection of revenues. Choice of the relevant individuals becomes itself a matter of very great significance, and often of controversy and violence. If an organization such as the United Nations is performing the function of global collective-good intermediation, then why should it not, and why does it not, obtain its revenues, like lower-level collective-good intermediaries, through taxes? One might say that in fact it does. The immediate source of funds has been "assessments" on member states or their voluntary contributions. Ultimately, however, the burden falls on individual human beings. Thus, in effect, national governments have been serving as tax collectors for the United Nations. At the same time, however, national governmental representatives have guarded jealously their discretion in making funds available to the UN or withholding them from it. Clark and Sohn (CS) have presented one of the best-known and detailed elaborations of a system incorporating taxation to support IO programs.

1. NATIONAL TAXES (CLARK-SOHN)

A principal objective of the CS proposal is "sufficient and reliable support" for international organizational activities. To this end, each member government would accept a form of strict collective responsibility calling for designation in advance of IO expenditure decisions of a percent of specified taxes assessed under the respective national codes. National governments would accept the entire administrative burden of collection. Borrowing would be allowed, but except for emergencies debts would be constrained to 5 percent of gross planetary product. Programs would be authorized by the General Assembly that would also pass upon cost shares for each budget. Cost shares would be assessed in proportion to gross world product with the qualification of a uniform per capita deduction of not less than 50 percent nor more than 90 percent of the per capita income of the ten members with the lowest average. A ceiling of 2.5 percent of GNP would be established for any particular national share.

Clark and Sohn propose an allocation of responsibilities and a procedure for preparing, submitting, and adopting annual budgets. Agencies would propose programs and request funds. A standing committee on budget and finance would review agency proposals and make recommendations to the General Assembly. The latter would vote on budgetary matters under a majority decision rule qualified to include a majority within the group composed of the ten members tentatively assigned the largest cost shares.

Clark and Sohn claim advantages for their proposal as follows. It would: (1) provide a reliable system for raising large sums; (2) avoid administrative expense of tax collection; (3) institute a direct relation between individuals and the organization; and (4) provide national autonomy in choice of taxes.

It is not clear at all that the system would in fact be characterized by an especially high degree of reliability. No sanctions can be applied. No leverage exists to facilitate extracting support from potential forced riders, who almost surely will search for means, undoubtedly easily available, to avoid at least part of the specified contribution. Thus, the CS proposal heavily emphasizes the obligation of membership, the familiar nemesis, collective responsibility, which experience has shown incapable of eliciting large sacrifices from unwilling decision makers.

The CS proposal does contain an attempt, in the form of qualifications to the majority voting rule,[3] to limit the severity of the problem by promoting a positive relation between benefit and sacrifice. But as demonstrated in principle by Buchanan and Tullock, if the scheme were to be implemented as formulated the distinct possibility would arise for representatives of a decided minority to legislate an onerous sacrifice on a substantial majority (pp. 220 ff.). Rather more likely, and also a substantial drawback,[4] would be legislation of forced rides for a considerable minority. Thus, this plan calls for surrender of sovereignty that carries with it the potential for financial tyranny imposed by an extremely remote, however well intentioned, group of persons who would have at their disposal authority to exact sacrifices from individuals whose means for communicating their relevant preferences would be extremely indirect and unconvincing. The temptation for high-handed exercise of power would be almost inevitable and the opportunities for individual redress from abuses by the remote authorities extremely limited. One might say that the scheme comes close to taxation without representation in the worst sense. Contributions would be coerced directly from individuals who would have only a very limited, indirect voice in choosing international organization authorities, let alone in guiding their decisions.

Superficially the major drawback of the Clark-Sohn proposal may appear to be that it is somewhat "ahead of its time," a premature attempt to apply taxation, the tried-and-true source of revenue for a multitude of collective-good intermediaries of lesser scope, on a global scale under rather unfavorable conditions. But it seems doubtful, too, that the mechanism they propose would necessarily be especially effective in attaining their primary objective. Furthermore, severe undesirable side effects, most notably forced riding, appear inevitable. Finally, a reliable system of revenue is not likely to be the only objective, and if it is heavily stressed, others, such as efficiency and equity, probably will suffer.

2. CONTRIBUTIONS BY GOVERNMENTS

A number of proposals call for greater stress on so-called voluntary contributions by governments. Under such proposals national governmental representatives explicitly will have the authority and responsibility for determining the size of contributions and the corresponding sacrifice by their constituents. There would be no advance acceptance, as a condition of membership, of cost-sharing scales determined through voting. These proposals also seek more dependable sources of revenue, but they emphasize the link between greater dependability and avoidance of gross disparities between distributions of benefits and of costs as perceived by national representatives.

The Irish resolution [5] of 1965 is a prominent example of this line of thought. It proposed that only those permanent members of the Security Council who voted in favor of an operation be asked to commit their constituents to the corresponding sacrifices. In effect avoiding responsibility for payment was no more difficult than simply abstaining from voting on an operation for which there was no special desire. The resolution also provided that any UN member or other state or organization may make voluntary subscriptions. Thus, the Irish resolution explicitly recognized the independence of at least some national representatives from financial responsibility simply on the grounds of membership. At the same time, it allows the organization to facilitate association of those who share desires for a program while avoiding unnecessary stimulation of opposition.

The Irish proposal did not, however, constitute a complete conversion to governmental voluntarism. Other components stressed the obligations of membership. All participating members were to be called upon to share, within what were essentially income categories,[6] in proportion to the scale established for the regular budget. Most governments, indeed all except permanent members of the Security Council, were not to enjoy the privilege of opting out, presumably on the ground that they were being called upon to accept only a relatively minor sacrifice in the first place. In essence, then, the Irish resolution was a compromise intended to find a new acceptable balance between strict collective responsibility and pure governmental voluntarism. The effects of implementing this proposal might be expected to reflect this compromise. Thus, propensity toward large deficits may have diminished principally because authorizations for expenditures would take into account the limitations on resources from nonparticipation. The potential remained, however, for smaller deficits due to the opposition from governments of smaller nations that would have been denied legitimate unilateral refusal to contribute.

The Irish plan also was not very well adapted to situations in which lower-income countries were parties to conflict, received a large portion of the benefits, and would be willing to bear the costs. Thus, like so many other proposals, the Irish plan set up a general-purpose assessment scale that may not have fit very well some important international security programs.

3. TAXES ON TRANSNATIONAL INTERACTIONS

Still another potential source of revenue, taxes on certain categories of transnational interactions, might be mentioned briefly. International travel and postal, canal, sea, and air traffic have been identified specifically (Stoessinger et al., p. 271). Conceptually, the rationale for such taxes in terms of benefits would appear to apply just as well to more prominent interactions such as those involving commodities, real capital, securities, and so on. Parties to all such transnational interactions benefit more from reduced risks of international disorder than do more casual users.

But it would nevertheless seem blatantly inefficient and unfair to request sacrifices from only a small percentage of all individuals who would benefit perceptibly from international security programs. If such programs were directed at providing security for, or otherwise facilitating, the specific activities, the case would be more convincing. As the sole, or major source of support for general globally shared programs, they suffer from the very clear defect of omitting the overwhelming majority of beneficiaries.

4. AGGRESSORS

Finally, some have suggested that the aggressors be called upon to pay (Stoessinger et al., p.p. 170-71). The proposal possesses strong emotional appeal. Aggression to the severe detriment of the victim seems to run counter to many long-standing and currently prevalent ethical and legal systems. The notion that victims of criminals ought to be compensated, perhaps through restitution by the perpetrators, seems plausible. Reparations have been an element in many peace treaties.

The great practical problem is, of course, identification of the aggressor,[7] if in truth there is one, and eliciting the appropriate response. The difficulties may not be as insurmountable as commonly supposed, and a special role for aggressors or potential aggressors is an important component of the proposal presented below.

5. BENEFICIARIES

Many of the proposed reforms focus much more heavily than heretofore on the distribution of benefits as a guide to workable distributions of cost share. Opting out and levies on international transactions clearly reflect this tendency. In a very practical way suggested measures of benefits do the same.

Thus, for example, setting shares proportional to assets in an area of potential conflict ties contributions to benefits in the form of reduced risk of loss of tangible capital (Stoessinger et al., p. 172). The intent seems to have been foreign-held assets. But if we accept greater attention to benefits as the real objective of the proposal, we should recognize that reduction of risk applies to all sorts of assets, foreign and domestic, tangible and intangible. That is, the domestic surgeon may have as much or more to lose from international disorders involving his country than the foreign owner of tangible capital. Wealth provides a more comprehensive measure than current income, presumably indeed reflecting present values of future income streams as well. But measures of intangible wealth, often by far the most important variety, are not well developed. Reliance on current income, which after all is related to wealth in some degree, seems likely to remain the more practical indicator for some time.

The suggested relating of cost shares to *national* security expenditures likewise can be rationalized in terms of greater stress on the distribution of benefits. Expenditures for national security programs presumably reflect a balance between perceived needs and the capacity to pay.[8]

Governments undoubtedly will remain reluctant to provide the data needed to assess accurately the comparative sizes of their national security budgets. Consequently, budgetary practices often will remain obscure, to say the least, thereby creating a serious obstacle to this approach. The idea does have sound elements, however, and we shall consider more carefully below the possibility of incorporating them.

Still another proposal with the apparent aim of linking more closely the distributions of benefits and contributions involves distributing votes more nearly in porportion to financial contributions. More votes to the larger contributors would guarantee their ability to guide programs in the direction conforming with their conception of the beneficial. Those unwilling or unable to contribute a substantial share would have a commensurately smaller role in determining the nature of the program and hence the distribution of benefits generated by it.

This line of thought can be extended to the ultimate locus of all contributions, namely, the individual human being. Each contributor might be granted influence on decisions regarding the nature of programs strictly in proportion to the command over resources he is called upon to sacrifice in their support. Thus, distributing votes according to financial contribution seems tantamount to a strictly economic determination of resource allocation. That is, the allocation would be exactly the same as if a collective-good intermediary responded efficiently simply to individual monetary ballots. Intuitively the equivalence seems highly likely, although it is not our purpose here to construct rigorous models to demonstrate it.

6. CONCLUSIONS

In sum, many of the proposals have in fact included elements that at least implicitly stress more heavily the importance of the distribution of benefits. The proposals as elaborated tend to be piecemeal, to focus heavily on the immediate problem of the UN deficit, to fail to link carefully more general objectives to the overall mechanism, and to pay at best very cursory attention to concepts and principles, even if controversial, from the general theory of sharing collective goods. Of course, all this in no way precludes a useful contribution that many of these ideas might make to a more comprehensive scheme.

Some proposals considered tactical as measured by the required adjustment to the existing mechanism might be regarded as strategic when viewed from the perspective of their consequences. For example, restricting expenditures to the sum of payments previously received may appear as a most elemental shift. Its consequence, however, would be elimination of deficits, a consequence that many observers of the UN of the 1960s and 1970s would regard as having strategic implications. Similarly, the cumulative impact of a series of "minor" changes may be greater than the simple sum of their separate impacts. Let us consider then a series of suggestions for improving UN financing that we might be tempted to label minor.

Certain proposals constitute essentially bargaining tactics to promote collective responsibility. For example, some analysts have urged that the so-called voluntary programs be included in the regular UN budget (Stoessinger et al., p. 210). The main effect clearly would be strengthening attempts at moral suasion for those happening to support programs under consideration. Reluctant contributors may respond in many ways, positively and negatively, to such demands. Another method suggested for applying pressure has been the maintenance of dual budgets, one at the "assessment level" and a second at the "spending level." Only the second is operational, the first serving mainly as a reminder of what might be accomplished if only all members would live up to their "responsibility."

Other suggestions call for promoting voluntary contributions through traditional techniques such as using the prestige and legitimacy of the secretary general's office to facilitate solicitations, devising matching formulas, or convening the assembly for announcement of pledges. Some hope to devise a formula indicating "fair shares," that is, "some objective formula by which governmental contributions would, while remaining nominally voluntary, follow an ascending curve on some agreed equitable basis" (Stoessinger et al., p. 214).

Still others focus on efficiency in the process of program choice. Thus, for example, budget coordination, or consolidation, has been propounded as an avenue to systematic, simultaneous consideration of the many alternative, often overlapping, programs involving global sharing. In this way trade-offs can be analyzed and decided upon systematically. Opportunities and the need for sacrifices can be juxtaposed and rational decisions facilitated.

Similarly, simultaneity in consideration of expenditures and in cost shares has been advocated on the grounds that account can thereby be taken of significant interdependencies. As we have seen, simultaneity also constitutes an important step toward constraining expenditures to amounts corresponding to the sum of acceptable cost shares and therefore toward avoiding deficits. The requirement for a more comprehensive agreement may tend to delay expenditure decisions and, in turn, programs, the outputs of which depend vitally on punctuality. To deal with this problem, capital funds might be established to cover initial vital efforts. Capital funds, too, will be evaluated as part of the proposal presented below.

B. Direct Personal Contributions: Costs and Benefits

Among the most interesting proposals for reform, especially from the viewpoint of contemporary microeconomics, is a more prominent role for personal contributions.[9] Voluntary individual contributions to UN peacekeeping have, nevertheless, been prohibited. This ban is curious, to say the least. To some it may seem almost incredible given the very wide range of other collective purposes to which individuals in many nations contribute without restriction. Yet the basic ban on private donations has continued ever since the creation of the UN.

What are the reasons for such an astounding contravention of individual freedom? Are the costs associated with voluntary individual payments likely to be so large relative to benefits that the extreme measure of overriding the fundamental principle of free consumer choice is clearly warranted? The remainder of this chapter is devoted to examination of broader costs and benefits of relaxing this remarkable ban.

Positions taken by governments on the acceptability of voluntary private contributions have tended to reflect assessments of their impact on the various national interests, and therefore during much of the post World War II period the Soviet government, understandably, has been a principal opponent. Furthermore, many national leaders have perceived voluntary contributions as contrary to their personal interests. Dictators and oligarchs especially may regard the idea that preferences of individual citizens should have a bearing on international affairs as laughable if not dangerous. In fact, most national leaders probably do not want their decision-making power in international affairs undermined by popular financing of peacekeeping. Even the American and British governments on occasion have displayed a clear lack of enthusiasm for it. In few cases, however, have governmental positions been supported by more than a cursory explicit consideration of the implications of private contributions, let alone a careful assessment of their net benefit. By far the most thorough and perceptive discussions of the pertinent issues are those of Professor Norman J. Padelford, and it is largely his analysis that provides a foundation for the present discussion.

1. STATEMENTS OF A THEME

Prominent among the disadvantages (or costs) attributed to voluntary private contributions to a United Nations peace and security fund is the idea that private support for international organizational "political" programs is somehow not "appropriate." This theme has been stated in several ways, all dealing with some aspect of the interrelationships among three distinct sets of decision makers: private individuals, national governmental authorities, and international organizational officials. To insure an accurate representation of the various expressions of the theme, they are quoted verbatim. Then they are discussed at some length in the remainder of the chapter:

". . . it has been the view at the Secretary-General level that political, and hence peacekeeping operations are the province of official decisions. It is felt that for the Organization to accept private gifts for such purposes . . . involve it in the moral position of having taken a commitment that could conceivably be at variance with the will of its Members" (Padelford, 10-26-62, p. 19).

". . . large amounts of money . . . would enable it to act independently of the will and payments of the Member States . . ." (Padelford, 10-26-62, p. 30).

Private individuals may attempt to "claim a voice in determining how and when . . . monies should be expended" (Padelford, 10-15-62, p. 12).

The UN ". . . exists for the purpose of serving the interests of states . . ." (Padelford, 10-26-62, p. 30).

"While gifts and donations have served special purposes and have been highly appreciated, nevertheless, it should be recalled that the United Nations is a public international organization. Not only are individual donations undependable, but special attention to this [independent] source of revenue would be a misconstruction of the principles and purposes of a general international organization. Ultimately support for the United Nations must depend upon the governments of the world or the peoples' of the world under international government with public responsibilities" (Commission to Study the Organization of Peace, pp. 259-60).

". . . a wholly voluntary fund would depart from the basic principle that peace and security are every Member's business and the fundamental *raison d'être* of the UN itself" (Padelford, 10-15-62, p. 12).

"The responsibility of states to support [the UN] . . . should not be undermined or diluted" (cited in Stoessinger et al., p. 160).

The first three propositions pronounce clearly the concern about implications of voluntary private contributions for the distribution of authority and responsibility for decision making among the three sets of individuals: private parties, national representatives, and international officials. With these issues apparently accorded quite heavy weight, Padelford has risked the clear-cut conclusion that the UN's "primary support for normal operating expenses and extraordinary peacekeeping activities should . . . come from states and not non-governmental sources" (10-26-62, p. 30). The essential conclusion that will emerge from the current analysis is quite different. It will be argued that these statements call attention to potentially important problems but that they do not constitute a clear-cut case for prohibition of private contributions. First, they fail to present a standard for an optimal distribution of authority and responsibility for decisions about international security programs. Second, they rely heavily on that vague concept, the will of member states. Third, they fail to admit that the international executive (IE) often would not make decisions at variance with the wills of heads of state and that in some circumstances if he did, a net benefit may be gained.

2. OPTIMALITY IN DISTRIBUTION OF AUTHORITY

The cited propositions only implicitly raise the question of the optimal distribution of authority and responsibility. They also display a curious asymmetry. Great concern is apparent for possible shifts in decision making away from national governments toward either an international organization or toward individuals. There is no acknowledgment of the possibility that the existing deviation from the optimal may be toward an excessive allocation of authority to national officials. Indeed, actual attainment of optimality in the past has not been argued, let alone satisfactorily demonstrated. Under the circumstances some reallocation of authority from member states or, more accurately, from the national governmental apparatuses toward individual human beings as well as toward the international executive quite conceivably, even probably, could be counted as a potential source of clear net benefit. What an extraordinary stroke of good fortune it would be if, quite by chance, we had stumbled upon and a fortiori continued along the path of an optimal division. In this light should we not ask for a more detailed explanation of what net benefits derive from avoiding undermining the position of member states through voluntary contributions. Are the benefits certain to offset the cost of violating the individual's freedom to contribute if he so desires?

3. RATIONALITY OF VIOLATING STATES' WILLS

The persuasiveness of the cited statements also is severely diminished by the very vague concepts they contain, particularly "the will of member states." Very special circumstances are necessary if this phrase is not to be virtually devoid of meaning. Presumably, the will of a member state reflects in some fashion the values of the various individuals within its jurisdiction and perhaps more specifically on particular issues the preferences of the persons holding positions in the national governments. Unless all individuals share a set of values identical in every detail, we cannot speak meaningfully of the collective will of any group of people independently of the method employed for aggregating their preferences. The phrase "will of member state" clearly stems from acceptance of elitism and the organic conception of the state discussed in Chapter II.

Given that the previously available assessments of the costs and benefits of a voluntary fund rely heavily on the concept of the wills of member states, it seems worth emphasizing that even if we can identify precisely such wills there may be many circumstances in which strict adherence to them may not be the course of action that many would regard as conferring the greatest net benefit. In any event, the preferences of the individuals comprising the national governmental apparatuses often will be so diverse as to reduce to impotence analysis founded on the concept of the monolithic will of member states.

The concern for a shift of authority away from national officials seems excessive, because in some situations it is unlikely that the international executive would make decisions at variance with the will of member states, and because in others if he does, a net benefit will be gained. Suppose, for example, that there was an unusual extent of agreement among the representatives of the national governments and that this consensus reflected the will of the peoples. In this situation a commitment by an international executive to a program, position, or activity of any kind contrary to the position of a national government would seem highly unlikely, especially if he had no institutionalized capabilities for compelling support in the form of taxation. In this circumstance the peoples would exercise their power of financial veto, and the IE's position would not be upheld.

Now, suppose the preferences of the national governmental apparatuses and those of the peoples diverge. A commitment by the IE in accordance with the peoples' views as opposed to those of the national governments may be regarded as a benefit of the system of voluntary contributions rather than as a cost.[10] One might expect in general some convergence between wills of governments and their constituents, either because of their more or less representative character, or because of officials' efforts to enlist support. But on occasion substantial divergences seem possible, and in these cases IE responsiveness to the will of peoples rather than to governments cannot be counted as an unmitigated cost, if a cost at all.

Still further circumstances can be imagined under which commitment in opposition to some states will generally be regarded as a benefit rather than as a cost. Suppose that hostilities between two member states appeared imminent. The remaining national governments and their peoples may count as benefits peacekeeping activities by the IE that would appear as costs to one or both of the adversaries.

Indeed, the very purpose of financing UN peacekeeping and peacemaking operations is to arrange programs for ameliorating and controlling conflicts among nations, that is, to divert the natural course of the relations resulting from their unconstrained interactions. In other words, an important benefit anticipated from UN activities is the modification and tempering of member states' wishes when their independent search for justice becomes excessively disorderly and expensive. From this vantage point commitments at variance with the wills of some national governments and perhaps even with their peoples as well may be generally regarded as a net benefit.

Still another aspect of the problem makes clear the probable costs in avoiding actions contrary to the wishes of some member states. Given the virtually universal incompatibility of such wishes, the refusal to adopt a position that in some minor way conflicts with that of any one implies adoption of no position at all. Never taking a position scarcely conduces toward maximizing net benefits for all concerned and implies on the contrary total abdication from any effort at adding to order in the interactions of nations. It permits, therefore, successive blockages, tyrannies by one minority after another.

4. PRIVATE INDIVIDUALS CLAIM VOICE

Finally, what can be said of the possibility that private individuals may attempt "to claim a voice in determining how and when monies should be expended"? In a sense, of course, if financing were completely voluntary, and if sizable donations were to be forthcoming, the aggregate of individuals would indeed have a predominant influence on the activities of the international organization, which, as we have seen, could even be regarded as essentially a collective-good intermediary. Then its main purpose would be to facilitate and to stimulate expression of the peoples' desires for international organizational programs and to arrange for their provision. The IE would be merely attempting to design and arrange for programs that the public regarded as of value.

Presumably concern is not with such claims by a multitude of individuals each with an imperceptible effect but with attempts by small groups to induce decisions to their own special advantage or in harmony with their own special outlook and ideology. A small private group may indeed attempt to gain influence in this fashion, but there are also many questions that might lead us to discount considerably this danger. How large a share would in fact be contributed by persons who realized and accepted that they would have an imperceptible effect on the character of international security programs? What shares would be contributed by the largest donors? Would donation of a large sum of money be the most effective means for private parties to acquire a voice? If large donations by a few contributors were to be limited to a certain share, what alternative means might they employ to use their wealth to gain their ends? Would the IE tend to be more susceptible to pressure from large donors or from nondonors who employed more subtle tactics such as covert maneuvering to influence choice of IO officials? Would the element of voluntarism and its threat of immediate suspension of contributions lead to greater resistance to private pressures on the part of administrators? What influence on the IE's decisions might be retained by national governments?

The question on the extent of dispersion in shares is crucial. Suppose that, as seems to be the case regarding general contributions for a variety of purposes, the overwhelming source of funds is a very large number of middle-income individuals.[11] For most such potential contributors adherence to the programs described at the time of contract,[12] or a very persuasive rationalization of deviations, would be the extent of the IE's obligation. Contributors could not be given a guarantee of results; nor is it likely that they would expect one. They could not even be guaranteed that the peacekeeping administrator would decide to take a particular line of action, or any action, in any given set of circumstances. The public would be assessing past performance with a view to determining the efficacy with which the administrator was handling his mandate, and it would adjust its offerings accordingly. Deviations by the IE to accommodate the preferences of a small minority at the expense of the general public may be accompanied by a decline in latent and therefore revealed demand. As at all levels of collective-good intermediation, confidence in the integrity of the intermediary will be an essential condition for inspiring willingness of the public to reveal even a part of its demand and to continue support for any particular individual in his post as intermediary.

Presumably the IE would prefer the situation of the large number of small donors because of the independence and trust conferred upon him by the financial vote of confidence of the many small donors, each recognizing and accepting his own imperceptible effect on total demand. Thus, the IE may propose measures such as the limitation on shares provided by any single individual or small group. But such a limitation does conflict with freedom of consumer choice, and since there may be considerable doubt, both with reference to the need for reliance on contributions of a small number of private individuals and to anyone's willingness [13] to contribute huge sums, it may be expedient for the IE to be alert to more positive evidence of an impending problem rather than to erect precipitantly a superfluous constraint.

Finally, a continuing role for national governments is compatible with the introduction of some elements of private voluntarism in funding international organizational security programs. The dominance of national governmental represenatives' influence on the IE relative to that of individuals manifest under existing institutions is not likely to be easily broken simply by granting authority to the IE to seek voluntary contributions, possibly limited, from private individuals.

Clearly, with or without private donations *some* expression of individual preferences and *some* attempt by private individuals to claim a voice on broad policy issues in international peacekeeping is inevitable. After all, under any set of institutions it is individual human beings who forgo other goods to pay for the services that the UN provides. The question is not if it should be private individuals who provide the financial wherewithal, but if they could and should provide it directly and voluntarily. If they do, the IE will be concerned with the general acceptability of his proposed programs; and especially if support is widely diffused, such catering to the "will of the peoples" could hardly be regarded as an unmitigated evil. There is no compelling case that institution of a voluntary mechanism for expressing demand for IOPOPJ would enhance possibilities for exerting private pressure for private gain, and it remains to be determined whether in fact the net effect may not be just the opposite.

5. UN EXISTS FOR STATES

Now, consider the assertion that the UN exists to serve the interests of states. This proposition also simply assumes optimality in the existing distribution of decision-making authority, particularly between member states and the UN. But don't the member states in turn exist to serve their respective peoples, and therefore doesn't the UN exist to provide a service ultimately to individual human beings? The initial phrase of the preamble to the UN Charter itself recognizes "peoples" as the ultimate source of its legitimization, stating: "We the peoples of the United Nations. . . ." If the UN ultimately serves the peoples, and if ultimately the peoples provide the resources that the UN requires, the permanent need for national governments as go-betweens seems doubtful.

Individual humans support provision for collective goods directly at various levels of jurisdiction. A careful explanation of the rationale for bypassing direct relationships seems highly desirable. The simple assertion that the UN exists to serve the interests of states clearly does not provide an elaboration of a net benefit that would offset the advantages of more direct communication and noncoercive relationships between the peoples and the organization attempting to provide for their collective needs.

6. UNDEPENDABILITY OF PRIVATE CONTRIBUTIONS AND NECESSITY OF GOVERNMENT

According to the Commission to Study the Organization of Peace, private contributions are undependable and constitute a misconstruction of the principles and purposes of a general international organization.

Such an organization must draw support from national governments or from peoples under world government. The case for such strong assertions is difficult to make with regard either to the whole or to any of its components. Indeed, the passage quoted is accompanied by no discussion whatsoever of the factors leading to undependability or of the reasons for supposing voluntary contributions would be more undependable than financing obtained through other mechanisms.

The bald assertion that donations will be undependable may be misleading, and in any event uncertainty is hardly peculiar to a voluntary and privately contributed fund. A priori attribution of a special degree of uncertainty to this particular method of finance seems clearly inaccurate, especially in light of the evidence that has accumulated demonstrating the very substantial uncertainties attending attempts to coerce reluctant governments to pay "assessments" for ongoing operations. In fact, attempts to coerce powerful and not so powerful national governments into paying "assessments" almost without doubt will produce a very substantial degree of uncertainty, probably even greater than that associated with a voluntary approach. With the benefit of hindsight, it now seems that few mechanisms could be much less dependable than ones actually employed in the past. Thus, supplementing governmental assessments with individual contributions quite possibly could yield a steady minimum well above historically observed UN revenues for international security programs. This is a factual matter about which great conviction in asserting conclusions hardly seems warranted. How large would contributions be, and what factors are likely to affect them? How will they vary from country to country? How large would donations be relative to the IE's statement of needs? What of the evidence that has been cited in support of the previously expressed speculations about a fund? What experiments might be most advantageous in providing additional evidence? We need much better answers to questions such as these.

Similarly the bald assertion that "support for the United Nations must depend upon the governments of the world or the peoples of the world under international government with public responsibilities" may very well be something of an overstatement. It is in effect an impossibility theorem ruling out voluntary collective action of individual human beings. In view of the quite extensive evidence cited above of considerable contributions to voluntary collective action, especially in the face of grave danger or disaster, the impossibility theorem seems entirely unwarranted. What is needed is a careful examination of effects associated with alternative mechanisms for financing an international organization's activities. Until such an examination becomes available, rejection of voluntary collective action out-of-hand constitutes an unwarranted restriction on the range of possible institutions.

7. PEACE AND SECURITY ARE EVERY MEMBER'S BUSINESS

Still another proposition in the case against private contributions claims that "A wholly voluntary fund would depart from the basic principle that peace and security are every member's business and the fundamental *raison d'être* of the UN itself." The underlying rationale seems to be that voluntary contributions would allow some member states to escape from their duty to contribute. Perhaps peace and security are every member's business, but does it really follow that each member must be expected to contribute to *every* program, especially in an amount determined largely by others?

As a practical matter, strict adherence to demands that all states pay for each and every IOPOPJ amounts to a requirement for unanimity that in practice rarely seems attainable and in all probability will lead to denial of any support at all. Ideally every member might be expected to accept more readily a commitment to certain types of program in the abstract and grant authority to the IE to use his judgment in specific applications. Even here the greatest net benefit might be derived through voluntary contributions that would reduce the risk of no programs at all because of insistence on an impractical unanimity requirement.

From a more general point of view, the strict interpretation of the principle that peace and security are every member's business seems to clash with another, perhaps more fundamental, namely the freedom to withhold support from an activity, operation, or agency for which one has no desire and of which one in fact actively disapproves. With these arguments in mind, we may well conclude that the escape from payment by certain members may on occasion constitute a substantial benefit of incorporating the element of voluntarism in the procedures for financing international security programs.

8. GOVERNMENTAL EXPERTISE

A plausible, though neglected, argument may be developed supporting emphasis on states' responsibility for decisions on financial support of the UN. Specifically, national governments provide a collective good to their constituents in the form of judgments about the desirability of alternative measures in the conduct of foreign affairs. Arriving at the necessary judgments is a highly specialized operation with many activities requiring a large organization of professionals in the national government. It might be argued, therefore, that governmental policymakers with their staffs of experts can make more rational and informed choices relevant to useful levels of financial support for international security programs than can the nonspecialist.

Although government officials indeed have been more knowledgeable on many matters dealing with foreign affairs, they also have been more deeply involved emotionally and more keenly aware of the conflicts between their objectives and those of other governments. They have become more directly parties to conflict and subject to the irrationalities that beset human beings when thus involved.

Furthermore, the public undoubtedly will be placed in the familiar position of being its own expert by having to choose among a rich menu of positions, advocated by highly competent analysts of international relations, including the IE. Thus, on balance it scarcely has been established definitively that decisions of national governments pertinent to their external relations can be regarded as inevitably superior, let alone that their expertise constitutes sufficient grounds for denying individuals an adequate mechanism for expressing the intensity of their opinions about the usefulness of international security programs.

9. CENTRALIZED AUTHORITY FOR TAXATION

The lack of authority and capability for raising revenues via taxation at the international level sometimes has been lamented or at least remarked upon with apparent regret. The central problem here is the very rationale for instituting a tax system, a complex issue that can only be mentioned at this time. But the consequences of granting authority to a single worldwide executive to use force both to preserve order and to compel financial support from individuals would appear to deserve very careful scrutiny. From the perspective of the early 1980s one can easily gain the casual impression that much evidence could be accumulated to demonstrate highly centralized governments' lack of responsiveness and abuses of power facilitated by the coercion that taxation constitutes. No extensive examination of this issue can be attempted here. It seems worthwhile, nevertheless, to call attention in this context to the possibility that a voluntary system of financing international security programs may have the considerable advantage of avoiding exaction of individual payments for undesired programs proposed by the ultimate in centralized authority.

10. EXACERBATION OF TENSIONS OVER CONTROL

Could financing that was more independent of national governmental decisions exacerbate tensions over control? According to Stoessinger et al., "the issue of control is the central political concern, and this issue would probably be more, rather than less, acute in the case of a financially independent United Nations" (p. 31).

With the problem of finance "solved," remaining items on the agenda of necessity would become the focus of attention. But further, with funds in hand the issue of how to control their expenditure would become of greater potential consequence to various "national interests," and a fund established over the opposition of one of the parties to conflict might risk aggravation of tensions to an extent more than compensating for the benefits that could be gained through expending the fund. Failure of an adversary to volunteer his "fair share" may lead to expression of his enemy's resentment through more than merely curtailing donations. Thus, any previously existing contention over control of the fund just might be intensified by its very creation.

These clearly are legitimate concerns, but can we really have much confidence that tensions arising in this fashion would necessarily be greater than those associated with other courses of action including the cumulative aggravations of failure to achieve an accommodation over the issue? Nations appear, ironically, to be more than willing to risk provocation of their antagonists by accumulating and brandishing military equipment capable of annihilating each other, while balking at the risk of provocation inhering in the establishment of an international voluntary peace fund.

Furthermore, some effects of the voluntary fund may tend to defuse the issue of control. The very delegation of any authority to the IE for expending voluntarily contributed funds would reallocate some decision-making authority from national governments toward individuals as well as toward the IE. Granting additional authority to the IE and to private individuals in effect tends to take some issues out of the hands of the national governments and perhaps consequently to remove some minor bones of contention thereby permitting them to focus on the larger issues. Quite conceivably, positions taken by smaller powers would find favor both with the IE and with a constituency of individuals in many countries while simultaneously at odds with adversary governments. Thus, a voluntary fund may be a subtle addition to the set of forces drawing adversary powers together in the face of opposition from the outside.

In sum, although creation of a voluntary fund may make the issue of control more "acute," the risks involved seem unlikely to exceed by much, if at all, those attendant upon continuing without more adequately financed services for peacekeeping and for ameliorating international conflict.

11. FISCAL AND POLITICAL IRRESPONSIBILITY

Still another view of costs that might be associated with the institution of a voluntary fund comes under the general heading of fiscal and political irresponsibility. That is, if nongovernmental contributions were to become very large, might they have the effect of allowing national representatives to vote for peacekeeping activities or appropriate money without having to count the cost or to account to constituents for their actions (Padelford, 10-26-62)?

There are reasons to believe that on the contrary voluntary private contributions may curb irresponsibility more effectively than assessments. The essential reason is the more direct link between the real burden bearers and the international peacekeeping executives. When governments "contribute," they have power to coerce taxpayers and therefore may feel less compulsion to provide commensurate services for the revenues they collect. Furthermore, since national governmental revenues cover a multitude of activities and programs, the bearer of a tax finds it virtually impossible to associate his outlays with any particular program or to voice directly and effectively his opposition to excessive spending on any he disapproves.

If individuals were to contribute voluntarily to a specific program such as peacekeeping, they may have a greater inclination to take interest in how the money is expended and to exert fiscal discipline by reducing their support if spending were to be flagrantly frivolous.

Clearly, the separation of control from responsibility for financing carries with it only the risk of irresponsible spending. To some extent, such separation inheres in arrangements for collective consumption generally, but rather than contributing to the problem, removal of coercive assessments might contribute significantly to its control.

12. RIVALRY WITH OTHER FUNDS

A final category of costs may be distinguished, namely, diminished contributions to other voluntary funds (Padelford, 10-26-62, p. 28). For individuals concerned with administration of and contributions to such alternative funds, leakage to a rival would indeed appear as a cost. To the extent that such a diversion in fact would occur, other charitable institutions have been subsidized by the prohibition of private contributions for UN peacekeeping services. But wouldn't the overriding consideration be freedom of an individual's choice, this time with respect to his response to the perceived urgency of the need for the various collective consumption goods?

13. FLEXIBILITY

Flexibility may be enhanced in the sense that establishment of a voluntary fund would not preclude or indeed interfere in any direct way with other possible modes of financing.[14] Thus, a broader range of alternative sources of financing would be available to those responsible for obtaining the economic wherewithal needed for international security programs.

Padelford has suggested that voluntary governmental contributions might help to avoid the need for "laborious diplomatic negotiations and possible stalemate in arranging a special scale" (10-5-62, p. 31). The same benefit would apply, of course, to individual contributions as well. Unlike a more coercive and restrictive mechanism, the voluntary fund avoids stimulating outright opposition of a marginally interested government, and a fortiori of a government negatively disposed toward the expected effects of a program.

A considerable advantage of a voluntary fund would seem to be that it would allow an effective means for expressing the virtually universally acknowledged desire for, and commitment to, international law and order in the abstract. As a matter of principle, some individuals may be willing to support measures for avoiding international violence, whereas in the "heat of battle" they may regard the international official as tantamount to a mortal enemy if he dares rule in favor of their opponents.

Furthermore, expression of preferences in this form would create a presumption of a relatively pure (untainted by considerations of national interest) demand, since contributors would be donating in advance without being sure that specific international peacekeeping operations would accord precisely with their individual desires. The argument might be extended even to the conflict between the partisans of change and those of the status quo, since again neither could be quite sure whether the fund would be used in favor of or against his interest.

14. AMELIORATION OF CONFLICT

A voluntarily contributed fund may have the virtue of allowing a mutual demonstration of concrete commitment to ameliorate and/or control international conflict more effectively. National governments, generally prone to distinguish between adversary governments and the corresponding population, may view funds provided voluntarily, with no strings, by individual citizens as less menacing and less suspicious than a fund supported largely via governments they regard as their potential enemies.

15. FREQUENCY AND INTENSITY OF RESORT TO VIOLENCE
AND MILITARY SPENDING

In counting the costs and benefits of admitting voluntarism in the expression of demand for IOPOPJ, an overriding consideration is the degree to which the objectives of reducing the frequency and intensity of resort to violence in international relations and of reducing the extent of diversion of economic resources to the various national military sectors would in fact be facilitated. But there is, of course, great uncertainty regarding the effects of establishing a fund. That is, where human conflict is concerned, prediction of the impact of a specific action or agreement on the sequence of subsequent events is especially difficult. Although knowledge of the effects of the fund can be only highly speculative, in its absence the level of international violence and of national military expenditures undeniably have constituted a major burden, and indeed a catastrophe for millions of individuals. It seems highly doubtful that voluntary donations permitting a greater role for an IE virtually devoid of national interest would contribute toward further disorder, accumulation of weapons, and resort to threats and to actual violence among nations. Some analysts of the international system argue, on the other hand, that there may be little that the IE could do to promote orderly pursuit of justice at the international level. Perhaps this view is correct, but it remains controversial at best. But again, it is not part of the present purpose to attempt a conclusion on this essential matter.

16. IMPACT ON SOCIETAL DEVELOPMENT

Important as preserving international order may seem, for some it may not be the overriding consideration. For them, one of the costs, and perhaps the dominant one, of an effective peacekeeper may be the tendency toward a slower pace of what they regard as social progress within some countries because of the peacekeeper's tendency to preserve the status quo.

On the other hand, oppressive domestic measures are sometimes found to be more tolerable and more tolerated when there is fear generated by a threat from outside the nation. If international authorities were more effective in ameliorating and controlling international conflict, national governments may find expedient greater responsiveness to the domestic needs and concerns of their respective constitutencies. Honest differences of opinion about the relative importance of these two tendencies also are likely to be debated for some time into the future.

In sum, the benefits and costs of a voluntary fund for international peacekeeping are quite difficult to establish. From the perspective of contemporary theories of public choice, prohibition of contributions for collective goods appears, nevertheless, as nothing less than extraordinary. *Overcoming* obstacles to expression of individual preferences, not erecting them, has been its primary objective. Thus, institutional obstacles to individual expressions of demand clearly are out of harmony with that fundamental foundation of modern theory, the individualist postulate, which emphasizes the vital role for each person in social decisions. Freedom of personal self-expression, although a basic human right, is of course not license to perpetrate fraud, slander, or other abuse. But is the prohibition of personal financial contributions to UN peacekeeping indeed a device to prevent potential abuses, or is it a device to prevent incursions into privileged preserves of national foreign policy elites? Most fundamentally, is the case for potential abuse sufficient to justify preemptive constraint on an essential human right? Surely answers to these questions will be profoundly pertinent to rational reform of institutions facilitating efficient global sharing under more nearly universally acceptable distributions of costs.

Notes

1. This summary draws on the work of the following: Grenville Clark and Louis B. Sohn, Joel Larus, President's Commission for the Observance of the Twenty-fifth Anniversary of the United Nations, Ruth B. Russell, John G. Stoessinger et al., United Nations Association of the United States, and David W. Wainhouse et al.

2. For some indications of its near universality, see Pryor and Musgrave (1969).

3. In the same vein, their plan explicitly "stops short of compelling membership by any nation."

4. In fact, one might speculate that in large part because of this obvious drawback, the scheme will not be accepted in the first place. The main purpose of this work is *not*, of course, to speculate on the acceptability of any set of arrangements or to predict the response of governmental representatives to any particular set of rules. The temptation to call attention to related implications is overwhelming, nevertheless. The Clark-Sohn scheme calls for national governments to accept the onus of collecting taxes while relinquishing the privilege of legislating programs to the general assembly. One is tempted to predict that national representatives will make no great haste to accept such a division of labor.

5. *United Nations Monthly Chronicle,* vol. 3 (January 1966), pp. 33-4.

6. Shares were to be allocated among income categories as shown in the accompanying table.

Category	Group Assessment (percent of total)
Less Developed	5
Developed other than Permanent Security Council member	25
Permanent Security Council members voting affirmative	70

7. It took years of intensive labor before the United Nations succeeded in developing a generally acceptable definition of the concept.

8. Determinants of national security expenditures could, of course, be analyzed in much greater detail. One determinant could be perception of effectiveness, or ineffectiveness, of *international* security programs.

9. Including those authored by the Irish government (resolution cosponsored by Ceylon, Costa Rica, Ghana, the Ivory Coast, Liberia, Nepal, the Philippines, and Somalia), Lincoln Bloomfield, Joel Larus, the President's Commission for the Observance of the Twenty-fifth Anniversary of the United Nations, and the United Nations Association of the United States.

10. One cost of a voluntary expression of demand by individuals may be stimulation of further efforts by national governments to control information flows to enlist support for their "will."

11. Inspection of data on the grant payments of leading American private foundations in the light of the total contributions raises considerable doubts that a few donors would be the source of a share large enough to persuade the IE to risk loss of support from a large number of other contributors (American Association of Fund-Raising Council, p. 14).

12. The time of contract refers to the period during which the IE presents proposed programs and individuals make their decisions about the level of support they are willing to provide.

13. Individuals wishing to influence IE decisions may allocate their funds to uses more directly serving their interests. Unconditionally releasing their financial means to a collective-good intermediary who is bound to pay heed to a large number of other uncoerced supporters may be far from the most effective means to influence decisions to gain pesonal ends. Direct prohibition may lead to attempts at subversion or to the next-best use of funds to gain those ends.

14. There may be indirect effects and interactions. If, for example, funds became available from other sources, governmental contributions or assessments, potential private donors may come to view their own contributions as less vital.

CHAPTER IX

A Microeconomic Perspective on Reform

Clearly there has been no dearth of proposals for reforming institutions and procedures governing decisions about international sharing. Much work, analytical and practical, nevertheless remains, to facilitate movement toward a solid consensus about their rational evolution. The conviction that the general microeconomic principles of sharing may contribute, perhaps even decisively, to such evolution has been a major inspiration for the current work. From this perspective, then, how might a proposal for reform be formulated?

As we have seen in Chapter III, public choice theorists have explored thoroughly two fundamental arrangements for collective goods, namely, voluntary exchange and tax-voting procedures. The voluntary approach risks attaining inefficiently low allocations because of free-riding but tends to avoid dissension, controversy, and conflict stemming from forced rides. Tax-voting mechanisms reduce the risk of free-riding but raise the potential for forced rides. The trade-off depends crucially upon a relatively little measured aspect of human behavior, that is, individual propensities to reveal latent demands for collective goods freely, only under special conditions, or only with a considerable understatement. Although contemporary theory emphasizes the lack of incentive to reveal latent demands for collective goods, the possibility of providing significant levels through essentially voluntary means cannot be ruled out.

Unfortunately, little direct evidence on the efficacy of voluntary individual contributions as a revenue-raising device for collective goods, global or otherwise, can be provided. The free-rider problem may be quite serious, even overwhelming. If so, the traditional economic approach would call for design and implementation of an international tax system to raise revenue.

At present, focus on the voluntary mechanism seems appropriate, nevertheless, for the following reasons. First, nationalistically inclined citizens, and especially officials, may be reluctant to accept the risk of commitment to taxes for support of global programs they do not want. Furthermore, pertinent programs proposed by intermediaries will tend to be tentative, cautious, exploratory, and limited in size. A phase of experimentation, learning, and groping toward more rational mechanisms will be required. Under the circumstances, limited moves toward the optimal allocation of resources to meeting global needs may be accomplished via voluntary support, even if some free-riding does occur. In the process much valuable additional evidence and understanding undoubtedly will be generated.

An example can show explicitly and relatively concretely how a voluntary mechanism might operate, what its consequences might be, the rules under which individual contributions would be allowed, and the influence they would have on policy decisions. Institutional arrangements, the general conceptual framework, and especially the behavioral hypothesis predicting responses to solicitations of voluntary contributions all are crucial elements of such an example. This is not meant to imply, of course, that we can project a precise sequence of institutional change and disregard the learning that presumably would occur throughout the process. We merely wish to demonstrate one way in which the general strategy of voluntary provision might be initiated.

For a conceptual framework we rely essentially on the contemporary theory of public microeconomics as elaborated in Chapter III. We emphasize that the weak free-rider hypothesis is consistent with some revelation of latent demands for collective goods and hypothesize further that individuals with intense desires will contribute, while others will not. We may be virtually certain, not only that revelations will fall short of the optimum, but also that some contributions will be forthcoming. Only experience can show whether they can finance programs of any significance.

As a practical matter, it seems doubtful that we will be able to determine even approximately the optimal level. We can suggest, however, that by the very act of contributing essentially voluntarily people reveal their preferences for that use of their funds relative to perceived alternatives. They, at least, would appear better off than if the option to contribute had not been available to them.

A. Expanded UN Role as Global Collective-Good Intermediary

Exactly how might the new institutional arrangement work, and specifically what will be the rules under which individual contributions will be permitted? The principal institutional innovation would be to allow the United Nations secretary general and his staff a limited expansion of their role as collective-good intermediary by accepting directly the voluntary contributions of individuals for specific international security purposes. The Secretariat would describe the programs for which it was soliciting contributions. It would explain the results achieved recently under previous similar programs, and it would set a target for anticipated need during the current period. Solicitation would take place under the auspices of the United Way [1] campaigns. Individuals would be permitted to earmark a portion of their United Way contribution for the proposed international security programs, to prohibit such an allocation, or to delegate responsibility to the campaign officers.

Individuals would be able to influence policy principally through their control of the purse. The Secretariat would be authorized to make proposals, but individuals would have to register their approval by making available the financial wherewithal. They would possess a major channel for influencing policy through, in effect, a financial veto. Presumably, the Secretariat would attempt to frame its proposals accordingly.

B. Limitation of Scope

To reduce the risk of massive unanticipated negative consequences, the scope of programs initially proposed by the Secretariat would be limited in a number of dimensions. First, a trial period would be specified at the outset. The period would be long enough to permit learning and removal of "bugs" from the procedures and short enough to avoid fears of excessive commitment or entrenchment. Approximately four years may be a workable compromise. Second, the experiment could be constrained initially to providing funds for limited purposes.[2] Thus, programs currently financed under existing procedures might continue to be so for the time being. Initial specific financial objectives might be attempts to: (1) eliminate the UN's accumulated deficit; (2) rebuild the Working Captial Fund; and (3) create a limited contingency fund for security programs.

C. "Fair Shares"

A vital aspect of the Secretariat's solicitation would be suggesting "fair shares," relying where possible on the distribution of benefits for their determination. Capacity to pay would be employed only to the extent that goods were judged normal, that is, that benefits were a positive function of income.

National security expenditures and participation in violent international conflict also would be treated as important information about the distribution of benefits. National security expenditures reflect a balance between benefits and costs attained within the various nations. Inasmuch as international security programs are regarded as at least partial substitutes for the national variety, the size of their benefits will be positively related. National participation in overt, violent international conflict also would be taken as prima facie evidence of special benefits accruing from substitution of an international security program. We shall return to a more detailed discussion of the rationale for these indicators below.

In sum, the viability of an essentially voluntary mechanism for financing globally collective goods could be investigated by recognizing and legitimizing the UN Secretariat's role as an intermediary, authorized to solicit contributions directly from individual human beings. A limited experiment could provide important evidence about the size of financial contributions achievable without taxation. At best, the result would be attainment of support closer to the optimal level. At a minimum, individuals would have an opportunity to express in a direct way, and in aggregate, effective way, their approval or their disapproval of the programs proposed by the Secretariat. Very important for protecting individual human rights is the fact that there would be ample opportunity for each person who disapproved to avoid making a donation. Solicitation involves suggesting fair shares based on much more information than simply capacity to pay relied upon so heavily in the past.

Although the next step toward rationalizing global sharing would be guided in part by the results of the first, some relevant considerations already seem evident. One direction would be to attempt financing programs for controlling and ameliorating specific, limited conflicts such as those in Cyrpus and the Middle East. Essentially the same mechanism might be employed, but further elements of a strategy for defining fair shares seem visible even now.

When a program is directed toward controlling a conflict between national governments, its benefits in the form of reduced risk of loss of assets, of life and limb, of close friends and relatives, and so on, accrue largely [3] to the citizens of the adversaries. On the other hand, the rest of the world has an overwhelming [4] share of the capacity to pay. As a first approximation, therefore, the costs might be divided equally between citizens of the warring countries and the rest of the world.

D. Estimating Personal Distribution of Benefits

How might the share of the adversaries be divided between them? Again, national security expenditures presumably would provide an indication of the benefits and costs of security programs perceived by individuals within the adversary countries and would provide guidance for establishing national contributions to the international variety.

A number of interesting effects may be anticipated under this approach. The aggressor, *and the victim,* insofar as the designations are appropriate at all,[5] would be called upon for a much larger share than under an essentially capacity-to-pay criterion. First, both would be requested to contribute heavily simply because of their involvement in the conflict. And, second, to the extent that large national security expenditures tend to be associated with more aggressive behavior,[6] the initiator of overt violence would be called upon for a relatively larger share.

The victims, or self-perceived potential victims, of aggression also would be asked to contribute more than under the simple guide of capacity to pay. Facing the possibility of greater immediate losses than the rest of the community, potential victims may regard contributions to an international security program, matched in part by persons from the aggressor nation as well as from the rest of the world, as an attractive alternative means [7] for promoting their own security.

Use of national security expenditures for such purposes may be objected to on the grounds of inadequacy and incomparability of relevant accounts.[8] And, indeed, national governments often have been exceedingly secretive and obscure where such accounting has been concerned. Useful data compiled by respected organizations such as the Stockholm International Peace Research Institute, the International Institute for Strategic Studies, the Brookings Institution, and so on, have been available for a number of years.[9] They already constitute the basis for a useful first approximation.[10]

As a practical matter, expediency may call for reliance upon concrete measures in physical units such as numbers of persons under arms, stocks of military capital items, and so on, aggregated in terms of compromise prices denominated possibly in terms of special drawing rights. Much relevant information already is published. The costs of refining it for the indicated purposes would seem relatively small. Whatever the deficiencies of this approach, it seems almost certainly to be far more satisfactory to sharing parties than reliance solely on capacity to pay.

In sum, certain characteristics of the distribution of personal benefits from national security programs seem more than clear enough to warrant use on at least a trial basis as a guide to global fair shares.

Many will be tempted to object, of course, that our hypothetical examples are hopelessly oversimplified by comparison with any actual situation. But the essential point is that the proposed mechanism takes account of much more highly relevant information than simply capacity to pay that has been relied upon so heavily in the past.

E. Role of Reserves

Our primary illustrative proposal suggested a contingency fund as a possible initial, limited goal. Indeed, contingency funds undoubtedly often will have an important role in global sharing, because specific needs arise suddenly with little advance indication. This fact has important implications for design of mechanisms aiming at efficient sharing. International programs in response to outbreaks of intergovernmental violence, to natural disaster, or perhaps to harvest failure [11] constitute major examples. Often a timely response can create net benefits very large relative to those associated with activities instituted at a more leisurely pace. The latter may fail to create benefits during the period of most urgent need. Furthermore, prompt response may forestall formation of conditions that lead to a larger stream of losses into the future. For example, controlling conflicts or epidemics of disease early may eliminate the risk of larger losses and/or the need for more expensive programs later. In such circumstances, how can the needs for rapid response, efficiency, and freedom of individual expression be reconciled?

The desirability of prompt response to emergencies creates a policy dilemma. Efficient allocation normally requires a flow of information from each consumer to the collective-good intermediary and its processing by the latter to determine the optimal program. Such flows and processing may require an interval incompatible with a response to emergencies, or to near emergencies, timely enough to be effective. To realize the relatively larger net benefits from a more rapid response, expediency will call for granting a specified discretionary authority to the collective-good intermediary. Efficiency will depend in part upon his ability to estimate accurately the distribution of individual benefits from the program. But in an emergency the gains from prompt action may overwhelm inefficiencies resulting from having little or no information regarding individual preferences pertinent to the specific situation.

One response to the dilemma stemming from the need to deal with emergencies is creation of a limited financial reserve. It can provide clear boundaries to the exercise of discretion by the intermediary, avoid deficits, yet provide for flexible response. Continuation of programs might be made contingent upon normal flows of funds from individual supporters. Even if support for a program does not materialize, the reserve will have to be replenished. Successive abortive initiatives presumably would tend to lower evaluations of the intermediary's performance.

The need for a reserve does not vitiate the logic of the main mechanism. The reserve merely provides an auxiliary to cope temporarily until the main mechanism can function normally. We might anticipate that as decision-making, collective-contract formulation, and data-processing capabilities rise, the need for the auxiliary mechanism may decline, but its elimination may be in the very distant future.

It is convenient to digress briefly at this juncture to note that reserves can perform another useful function, namely to smooth fluctuations, random or systematic, in voluntary flows of funds. One of the most emphatic and persistent criticisms of voluntary financial mechanisms is that their instability makes effective program planning virtually impossible. Elmandjra, for example, discussing assessments on governments as opposed to their voluntary contributions, writes:

> The concept of planning is very hard to accommodate with one of voluntarism. If one may make an analogy with resource allocation at the national level, the devising of international economic and social development plans to be financed principally from voluntary funds instead of assessed budgets is comparable to the elaboration of national economic plans whose financing is predominantly from foreign sources instead of from the national income. (p. 245)

In fact, greater instability has not been established. Inspection of Elmandjra's data showing growth rates of expenditures financed from assessments on governments as opposed to voluntary governmental contributions is hardly conclusive (p. 244). A chart showing trends in total expenditures creates a rather different impression (p. 241).

The main point, however, is that variation per se is neither an unmitigated evil nor especially costly to ameliorate. If, for example, variations in contributions were to correspond to variations in the latent individual demands, efficiency in the sense of meeting consumer needs would be promoted. Revenues should be available to take advantage of any excess of program benefits over costs. But when there are no such opportunities, revenues should decline commensurately. Furthermore, if administrators of programs find fluctuations disruptive, reserve funds might be used to smooth them out. Surges in contributions can be used to augment reserves rather than immediately to initiate new programs.[12] Ongoing projects threatened by lagging contributions can be completed by drawing down reserves. In this way a compromise might be achieved between the need for the guidance provided by individual expressions of preferences and the need for continuity in the implementation of programs. Declining reserves would serve as clear indicators of the need to limit expenditures.[13] Thus, it would appear that existence of voluntarism may not make planning nearly so precarious as often has been supposed.

F. Participation in Administration

The results of an experiment in voluntary global sharing along the lines described in our example may depend to a significant degree upon the administrative mechanism employed. Participation by the Secretariat's financial section is inevitable, but the extent of participation is an open question. It could range from minimal coordination with operational agencies such as national revenue services or United Fund administrations to full responsibility for all phases of the fund-raising process. Despite limited experience in global sharing, some speculation regarding the effects of alternative mechanisms may be worthwhile.

Cooperation of national revenue services may be very helpful in some respects. Substantial start-up costs could be avoided, especially those associated with acquiring an experienced staff. Indeed, sharing of facilities under conditions of ongoing operations also may reduce costs. Use of national revenue services would not be without drawbacks, however. The goal of an alternative channel for expression of individual preferences may be jeopardized by so close an association with the national revenue services, the leaders and employees of which may not be especially enthusiastic about cooperating with a weak rival collective-good intermediary with global pretensions. A further disadvantage may be inexperience with *voluntary* collective mechanisms.

Placing complete responsibility on the UN's financial staff would seem to imply a very substantial expansion in its size, justifiable on efficiency grounds only if there were to be great confidence that the results of the experiment would warrant institution of additional programs for global sharing. Then the investment in learning conceivably could be repaid by greater efficiency in providing the subsequent larger flow of services of collective-good intermediation.

The assistance of an international nongovernmental organization such as the International Red Cross could be very useful. A virtually global network of personnel experienced in securing voluntary individual contributions already exists, so that heavy start-up costs would be avoided. The Red Cross, because of repeated response to emergencies, is accustomed to dealing with novel programs of limited duration. A reputation of concern for individuals regardless of race, nationality, or ideological persuasion may be an asset for intermediaries attempting to arrange a limited experiment in global sharing. Of course, the details of cooperation between the Secretariat and others will have to be decided based upon the special knowledge and the discussion and negotiation of the parties involved.

The experiments described above, if successful, presumably would be a prelude to more ambitious undertakings involving choices among a variety of globally collective goods along with the whole gamut of private and less extensively shared collective goods that often are included in individual preference functions. Concurrent consideration of the full range of alternative uses of the individual's income corresponds, of course, to the approach of the orthodox neoclassical analysis. Granted the neoclassical approach often focuses on private goods only, but the extensions to sharing [14] are well known.[15]

Under the more realistic and complex circumstances, the role of the global intermediary will be to facilitate both rational individual sacrifices of nonglobal goods and rational choice among alternative globally collective goods. Information about needs, programs to meet them, suggested sources of support, and appropriate terms to promote trust and cooperation among those from whom the sacrifices of other goods must come will be among the functions of the intermediary. The complexities of performing these functions undoubtedly will multiply with the expansion of scope. A great deal of learning by experience will be necessary. Again it would seem premature to spell out details of subsequent experiments before the results of the initial one are available. The GCGI would be functioning in a fashion at least in some ways similar to the administrators of earlier transnational voluntary programs, and very likely could learn as they have learned.

Notes

1. Where no United Way exists, solicitation would be made through the International Red Cross or the national revenue services. Details would have to be

arranged by financial officers of the organizations involved. It is interesting to note that the Wisconsin State Employees combined campaign of 1976 provided for international sharing through CARE, Project Hope, the International Rescue Committee, Save the Children Federation, the American Kor-Asian Foundation, and Planned Parenthood-World Population.

2. It might be of interest to attempt generation of revenues for purposes where previously used mechanisms have created the well-known crisis.

3. Largely, yes, but of course not entirely. Many persons outside the zones of probable military operations may perceive benefits in the form of reduced risks of their own national forces being drawn into active participation in the conflict. Humanitarian motives, or interdependence of preference functions, if you will, may constitute sufficient grounds for the existence of latent demand outside immediate danger zones.

4. In the post-World War II decades this statement would have applied fairly well to any pair of adversaries not including the United States. By the 1980s the main thrust of the argument remains intact, even if the adversaries were to be the United States and another major economic power.

5. Sharing in the suggested fashion constitutes an approach similar to no-fault settlements by parties to civil conflicts. There would be no need to accomplish the delicate, to say the least, tasks of identifying just who the "guilty" party might be and of inducing acceptance of both the stigma and the burden necessary under the strict requirement that the "aggressor" foot the entire bill. The mechanism of course also provides further incentive to create an impression, whether through fact or fancy, of reduced national security expenditures.

6. We can only hypothesize here a tendency toward *some* relationship between national security expenditures and aggressiveness. Such expenditures also may be a function of capacity to pay. Aggressive behavior might be provoked by poverty, that is, limited capacity to pay, and so on.

7. Particularly by comparison with "going it alone."

8. A question might also be raised regarding possibilities of divergence between national security capabilities and national security expenditures. Capabilities may be more reliably linked to aggressive tendencies, whereas expenditures may more reliably reflect the civilian opportunities forgone.

9. A number of countries with large national security budgets do reveal extensive data that undoubtedly would be very enlightening for the proposed purposes.

10. Preparation of comparable current and historical accounts for national security expenditures may be a regular function of the international organization.

11. Even a cursory consideration of these examples suggests, of course, that the absence of indications may vary along a continuum. Adversaries can be relied upon to attempt surprise, although some signs may be discerned well in advance of overtly hostile activities. Similarly, indications of harvest failures, earthquakes, and so on may or may not be detected well in advance of the event, and of course, the extent to which they are is a function of resources and technology available for the effort.

12. The statement applies, of course, to programs required to meet persistent needs, not to the emergencies described earlier.

13. Restrictions on the extent of such funds would serve to limit the extent of slack in the reins running from individuals to the CGI.

14. Potentially all goods over various sets of individuals, up to and including the entire community.

15. See Buchanan.

CHAPTER X

Conclusion

In order to highlight the relationships between the main strands of our thesis, let us juxtapose its strategic elements.

A new, relatively neglected form of transnational economic interdependence is emerging, namely the interdependence associated with an existing potential for sharing globally collective goods. Rational choice in such sharing will require development of relevant normative and behavioral concepts and principles so that the confidence with which institutions and mechanisms are linked to objectives can be enhanced.

In the past international cost sharing, like national cost sharing before it, has been regarded as a province for "political" analysis and decisions. But just as the contribution of economic analysis to rational choices involving less comprehensive sharing has become more and more evident, so its potential for contributing to rational choices pertinent to global sharing is now emerging very clearly.

The individualist postulate constitutes a vital foundation for neoclassical economic analyses of sharing. Acceptance of this postulate implies an explicit rejection of the organic conception of the community. It emphasizes, rather, that individual human beings benefit from the creation of collective goods, and they also make the sacrifices necessary if such goods are to come into being. A model of rational choice can be based upon these essential premises, and clear implications can be derived for the mechanisms to be employed.

Concepts and principles from the general theory of collective goods can contribute to rational sharing of the global variety. The contemporary orthodox theory suggests that rational sharing is associated with certain properties of goods, namely nonrivalness in consumption and nonexcludability. It also permits precise description of the conditions that would prevail if an efficient allocation were to be attained. It warns of the lack of incentives for individuals to reveal their evaluation of benefits, and of the consequent difficulty in obtaining that vital information.

An emerging alternative to the orthodox doctrine suggests that the inevitability of such lack of incentive probably has often been overstated. Accordingly, it is entirely possible that terms of offer can be arranged such that, if latent demand exists, significant, though perhaps not strictly optimal, contributions may be expected. In this view, the standard conclusion that tax-voting mechanisms are essential for facilitating sharing underemphasizes the risks of forced riding, that is, exaction of sacrifices in support of programs in which no benefit is perceived.

Traditional approaches to international cost sharing have stressed ability to pay as the fundamental criterion for contributions. Many technical difficulties plague determination of ability to pay, but perhaps more important, such focus involves a most serious conceptual flaw, namely neglect of the distribution of benefits. There can be little doubt that parties negotiating a sharing agreement eventually will attempt to avoid accepting an assessment based simply on ability to pay if it violates their conceptions of efficiency and equity. Such conceptions will be based upon their perception of the distribution of net benefits rather than simply upon ability to pay.

The United Nations organization provides, of course, the foremost examples of global sharing. The notorious problems and controversy generated with regard to its financing might be viewed as a series of skirmishes in the cold war in which the disagreement of the adversaries was bound to create financial disarray. But a fairly persuasive case can be made that two interdependent fiscal procedures—collective responsibility of sovereign states and lack of simultaneity of budget determination—interacted almost inevitably to create a financial hobble for the organization. Where moderately large expenditures are involved, this interaction can be counted upon to create dissension and deficits, even if the sharers are not nationalistic and ideological opponents. The deficiencies of the basic approach were confirmed also by the experience of the specialized agencies.

Some proposed remedies for the organization's financial problems have emphasized alternative revenue sources, including direct taxes, taxes on transnational exchanges, voluntary contributions decided by national representatives or by individuals, and restitutions by aggressors. Others call for greater focus on benefits as indicated by assets in an area of potential or ongoing conflict or by *national* security expenditures.

Analysis of general collective-goods theory, of experience with international cost sharing, and of proposed remedies provides a basis for formulating a new experiment to test a mechanism aimed at promoting efficiency, equity, and individual freedom in global sharing.

The basic elements of this experiment include expansion of the UN Secretariat's scope of activity as a global collective-good intermediary. That is, the Secretariat would be authorized to propose programs creating essentially global collective goods and to solicit financial support for them directly from individual members of the world community. Thus, individuals would be free to express their support, if any, for globally collective goods in the most meaningful way possible (for the vast majority in any event), that is, through financial contributions.

The Secretariat may rely initially upon existing organizations, such as United Way campaigns, national revenue services, or the International Red Cross, for administrative services. Mechanics of eliciting responses will have to be studied in detail, and learning by the intermediaries undoubtedly will play an important role in the progression toward more effective procedures. In particular, individuals in all probability will desire some indication of what constitutes their fair share. Again, perceptions of the distribution both of benefits and of capacity to pay will play an important role.

Evidence currently available indicates that a substantial latent demand may exist for a most significant globally collective good, namely, international security programs. Furthermore, a consequential level of demand may be revealed if the prohibition against it contrived by certain national governments were to be removed. Aggregate American contributions for various purposes suggest strongly that preferences for collective goods sometimes are expressed to an economically significant degree. Opinion polls seem to indicate the possibility of a large latent demand for United Nations peacekeeping operations, and the declarations of national officials about the acceptability of a United Nations peace and security fund point in the same direction.

Nevertheless, in the past even respected Western analysts have voiced grave doubts about the "appropriateness" and general advisability of voluntary individual contributions for international peacekeeping purposes.

A careful review of the relevant arguments reveals many pros and cons. Issues include: the optimal division of authority and responsibility for decision among international officials, national officials, and the universal set of individuals; efficacy of negotiations by elites; exacerbation of tensions over control; fiscal and political irresponsibility; amelioration of conflict; channels for individual expression of desire for international order; frequency and intensity of resort to violence and military spending; and impact on societal development. Clearly, there are many imponderables. Individuals may place greater or lesser emphasis on alternative goals. Judgments will differ regarding the mechanisms most felicitous for attaining them. But precisely under such circumstances, freedom for alternative means of expressing individual preferences, including voluntary financial contributions, may be vital. Permission for individual contributions would enhance freedom of individual expression, so prominent in the United Nations Charter and the Delcaration of Human Rights, the positive scientific investigation of demand for globally collective goods, and progress toward rationality in global sharing.

References

American Association of Fund-Raising Council. *Giving USA: 1973 Annual Report.* New York, 1973.

Baumol, W. J. *Welfare Economics and the Theory of the State,* 2d ed. Cambridge, Mass.: Harvard University Press, 1965.

Becker, G. S. "Crime and Punishment: An Economic Approach." *Jour. Pol. Econ.,* 76 (March/April 1968): 169-217.

Bergson, A. "The Comparative National Income of the USSR and the United States." In D. J. Daly, ed., *International Comparisons of Prices and Output.* New York: National Bureau of Economic Research, 1972.

Bloomfield, L. P. Letter to the *New York Times,* February 25, 1962.

Bohm, P. "Estimating Demand for Public Goods: An Experiment." *Eur. Econ. Rev.,* 3 (June 1972): 111-30.

———. "An Approach to the Problem of Estimating Demand for Public Goods." *Swed. Jour. Econ.* (March 1971): 55-66.

Brubaker, E. R. "Free Ride, Free Revelation, or Golden Rule?" *Jour. Law and Econ.,* 18 (April 1975a): 147-61.

———. "Individual Values and International Security Programs." *International Organization* (Spring 1975b): 487-500.

Buchanan, J. M. *The Demand and Supply of Public Goods.* Chicago: Rand McNally, 1968.

Buchanan, J. M., and Tullock, G. *The Calculus of Consent* (paperback ed.). Ann Arbor, Mich.: The University of Michigan Press, 1965.

Chapman, J. G. "Consumption." In A. Bergson, and S. Kuznets, *Economic*

Trends in the Soviet Union. Cambridge, Mass.: Harvard University Press, 1963.

Clark, G., and Sohn, L. B. *World Peace through World Law,* 2d ed. Cambridge, Mass.: Harvard University Press, 1960.

Clarke, E.H. "Multipart Pricing of Public Goods. *"Public Choice,"* 11 (Fall 1971): 17-33.

Commission to Study the Organization of Peace. *Strengthening the United Nations.* New York, 1957.

Davis, L. E., and North, D. C. *Institutional Change and American Economic Growth.* Cambridge, England: Cambridge University Press, 1971.

Demsetz, H. "The Private Production of Public Goods." *Jour. Law and Econ.* 13 (October 1970): 293-306.

Dosser, D. "Allocating the Burden of International Aid to Less Developed Countries." *Rev. Econ. and Stat.* (May 1963): 207-09.

———. "Towards a Theory of International Public Finance." *Kyklos,* vol. 16, no. 1 (1963): 62-80.

———, and Peacock, A. T. "The International Distribution of Income with Maximum Aid." *Rev. Econ. and Stat.* (November 1964): 432-34.

Douty, C. M. "Disasters and Charity: Some Aspects of Cooperative Economic Behavior." *Am. Econ. Rev.,* 62 (September 1972): 580-90.

Dreze, J. H., and de la Vallee Poussin, D. "A Tatonnement Process for Public Goods." *Rev. Econ. Stud.,* 38 (April 1971): 133-50.

Elmandjra, M. *The United Nations System.* Hamden, Conn.: The Shoe String Press, 1973.

Fusfeld, D. R. *Economics.* Lexington, Mass.: D. C. Heath, 1972.

Gallup Management Research, Inc. *Gallup Opinion Index, Report No. 65, United Nations.* Princeton, N.J.: November 1970, pp. 9-11.

Gilbert, M., and associates. *Comparative National Products and Price Levels.* Paris: Organization for European Economic Cooperation, 1958.

Groves, T., and Ledyard, J. "Optimal Allocation of Public Goods: A Solution to the 'Free Rider Problem.' " *Discussion Paper No. 144,* The Center for Mathematical Studies in Economics and Management Science, Northwestern University, May 1975.

Head, J. G. *Public Goods and Public Welfare.* Durham, North Carolina: Duke University Press, 1974.

Herber, B. P. "The Public Sector in an Open System." In *Modern Public Finance,* rev. ed. Homewood, Ill.: Richard D. Irwin, 1971.

Katzenstein, P. J. "International Interdependence: Some Long-term Trends and Recent Changes." *International Organization,* vol. 29, no. 4 (Autumn 1975): 1021-34.

Knorr, K. *Power and Wealth.* New York: Basic Books, 1973.

Kravis, I. B., and Davenport, M. W. S. "The Political Arithmetic of International Burden-Sharing." *Jour. Pol. Econ.;* 71 (August 1963): 309-30.

Larus, J. *Liquidating the UN's Peacekeeping Arrears.* New York: New York University Center for International Studies Policy Paper, 1968.

Margolis, J., and Guitton, H., eds. *Public Economics.* London: International Economic Association, 1969.

Mishan, E. J. "The Relationship between Joint Products, Collective Goods, and External Effects." *Jour. Pol. Econ.*, 77 (May 1969): 329-48.

Mueller, D. C. *Public Choice*. New York: Cambridge University Press, 1979.

Musgrave, R. A. *The Theory of Public Finance*. New York: McGraw-Hill, 1959.

————. *Fiscal Systems*. New Haven, Conn.: Yale University Pess, 1969.

————. "Provision for Social Goods in the Market System." *Pub. Fin.*, 26 (1971): 304-20.

————, and Musgrave, P. B. "International Public Finance." In *Public Finance in Theory and Practice*. New York: McGraw-Hill, 1973.

————, and Peacock, A. T., eds. *Classics in the Theory of Public Finance*. New York: St. Martin's Press, 1967.

Neale, A. D. *The Flow of Resources from Rich to Poor*. Occasional Papers in International Affairs, No. 2, Center for International Affairs, Harvard University, November 1961.

Olson, M. *The Logic of Collective Action*, rev. ed. New York: Schocken Books, 1971.

————, and Zeckhauser, R. "An Economic Theory of Alliances." *Rev. Econ. and Stat.* (August 1966): 266-79.

Padelford, N. J. "The Financing of Future Peace and Security Operations under the United Nations" (mimeo). Cambridge, Mass.: 10-15-62.

————. "Private Support of the United Nations" (mimeo.). Cambridge, Mass.: 10-26-62.

Pfaff, M., and Pfaff, A. "Grants Economics: An Evaluation of Government Policies." *Pub. Fin.*, 26, no. 2 (1971): 275-303.

Pincus, J. A. *Economic Aid and International Cost Sharing*. Baltimore: The Johns Hopkins University Press, 1965.

Price, J. E. "The 'Tax' Burden of International Organizations." *Pub. Fin.*, no. 4 (1967): 496-513.

Pryor, F. L. *Public Expenditures in Communist and Capitalist Nations*. Homewood, Ill.: Richard D. Irwin, 1968.

Report of the United States President's Commission for the Observance of the Twenty-fifth Anniversary of the United Nations. Washington, D.C.: Government Printing Office, 1971.

Rosenstein-Rodan, P. N. "International Aid for Underdeveloped Countries." *Rev. Econ. and Stat.* (May 1961): 107-38.

Russell, R. B. *The United Nations and United States Security Policy*. Washington, D.C.: The Brookings Institution, 1968.

Russett, B. M., and Sullivan, J. D. "Collective Goods and International Organization." *International Organization*, 25 (Autumn 1971): 845-65.

Samuelson, P. A. "The Pure Theory of Public Expenditures." *Rev. Econ. and Stat.*, 36 (November 1954): 387-89.

————. "Diagrammatic Exposition of a Theory of Public Expenditure." *Rev. Econ. and Stat.*, 37 (November 1955): 350-56.

Schelling, T. C. "International Cost-Sharing Arrangements." *Essays in International Finance* (No. 24). Princeton, N.J., September 1955.

"Selected Bibliography of Literature on World Politics and International Economics." *International Organization,* vol. 29, no. 1 (Winter 1975): 343-52.

Singer, J. D. *Financing International Organization.* The Hauge, Nijhoff, 1961.

Skjelsbaek, K. "The growth of INGO in the 20th Century." *International Organization,* vol. 25, no. 3 (1971).

Smith, V. L. "Experiments with a Decentralized Mechanism for Public Good Decision" (mimeo.). Tucson, Arizona, June 1978 (forthcoming in the *Am. Econ. Rev.).*

Steiner, P. O. "The Public Sector and the Public Interest." In R. H. Haveman and J. Margolis, eds., *Public Expenditures and Policy Analysis.* Chicago: Rand-McNally, 1970.

Stockholm International Peace Research Institute. *Yearbook of World Armaments and Disarmament.* New York: Humanities Press, 1970.

Stegenga, J. A. *The United Nations Force in Cyprus.* Columbus, Ohio: Ohio State University Press, 1968.

Stoessinger, J. G., et al. *Financing the United Nations System.* Washington, D.C.: The Brookings Institution, 1964.

Tanzi, V. "A Note on Exclusion, Pure Public Goods, and Pareto Optimality." *Pub. Fin.,* 27, no. 1 (1972): 76-78.

Taubenfeld, R. F., nd Taubenfeld, H. J. "Independent Revenue for the United Nations." *International Organization,* vol. 18, no. 2 (1964).

Tideman, T. N. and Tullock, G. "A New and Superior Process for Making Social Choices." *Jour. Pol. Econ.* 84 (December 1976): 1145-60.

Tullock, G. "Public Decisions as Public Goods." *Jour. Pol. Econ.,* 79 (July/August 1971): 913-18.

United Nations Association of the United States. *The United Nations in the 1970's.* New York, 1971.

U.S. Bureau of the Census. *Statistical Abstract of the United States 1971.* Washington, D.C.: Government Printing Office, 1971.

Wainhouse, D. W., et al. *International Peacekeeping at the Crossroads.* Baltimore: The Johns Hopkins University Press, 1973.

Weiner, R. "The USSR and UN Peacekeeping." *Orbis,* 13 (Fall 1969): 915-30.

Weisbrod, B. A. "Toward a Theory of Relationships between Economic Sectors: Governmental, Private For-Profit and Voluntary" (mimeo.). Madison, Wis., 1972.

Wicksell, K. "A New Principle of Just Taxation." In R. H. Musgrave and A. T. Peacock, eds. *Classics in the Theory of Public Finance,* New York: St. Martin's Press, 1967.

Wolozin, H. "Volunteer Manpower in the United States." *Federal Programs for the Development of Human Resources.* U.S. Congress, Joint Economic Committee, 1968.

Index